Out of Line and Offline

THE PRIDE LIST

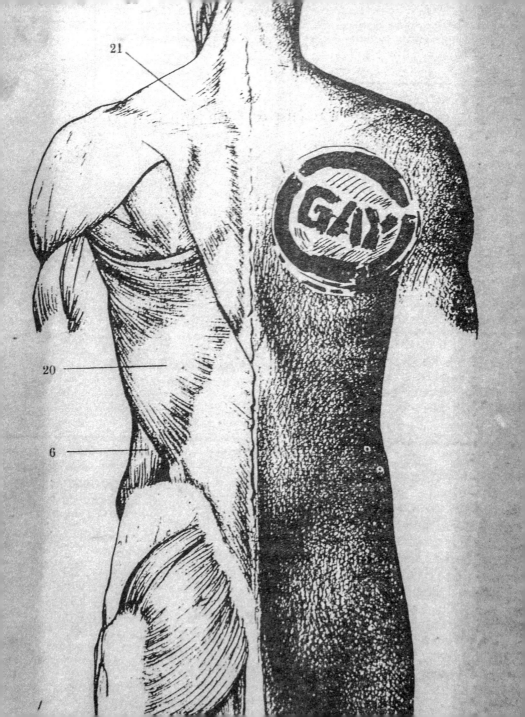

Out of Line and Offline

QUEER MOVEMENTS IN '90S EASTERN INDIA

Pawan Dhall

LONDON NEW YORK CALCUTTA

THE PRIDE LIST

EDITED BY SANDIP ROY AND BISHAN SAMADDAR

The Pride List presents new as well as classic works of queer literature to the world. An eclectic collection of books of queer stories, biographies, histories, thoughts, ideas, experiences and explorations, the Pride List does not focus on any specific region, nor on any specific genre, but celebrates the fantastic diversity of LGBTQ+ lives across countries, languages, centuries and identities, with the conviction that queer pride comes from its unabashed expression.

Seagull Books, 2020

© Pawan Dhall, 2020

Photographs and artworks © Individual photographers/artists wherever mentioned. Other images © Pawan Dhall / Varta Trust

ISBN   978 0 8574 2 743 4

British Library Cataloguing-in-Publication Data
A catalogue record for this book is available from the British Library

Typeset and designed by Bishan Samaddar, Seagull Books, Calcutta, India
Printed and bound by Hyam Enterprises, Calcutta, India

FRONTISPIECE. Image from front cover of *Pravartak*, July–December 1994 issue. *Artwork by Tia.*
PAGE iv. Letters from Counsel Club's files maintained by Varta Trust.

Contents

wan,

Hi, I am terribly sorry for
saying, 'Goodbye', before I left.
t, everything happened very fast.
– Calcutta, left my job, got
v one & etc etc. Anyway,
finally come back 'Home'.

22-12-98

199

1 on 26/2/98.
SNJB, NIR. SV
it to CALCUTTA
'99

Out of Line and Offline

Introduction

This story, or collection of stories, traces the impact that the earliest years of queer[1] activisms in eastern India had on people's lives. It documents the life stories of a few queer individuals and their allies who lived in the region in the 1990s or still do, and were influenced by the nascent community mobilization efforts of those years.[2] But a few caveats. The story does not dwell at length on what factors led to the queer movements

1 The term 'queer' includes lesbian, gay, bisexual, transgender, hijra, kothi, intersex as well as people who may identify differently, or with no such 'political' term at all, though their sense of gender, gender expression, sexual attraction, sexual behaviours or even sexual/romantic relationships are anything but heteronormative. These terms should, however, not be seen as 'categories' into which people can be conveniently bracketed. Moreover, in the Indian context, using gender or sexual-identity terms with Western roots as blanket expressions may be problematic. For instance, 'transgender', 'trans women' or 'trans men' may not be easy translations for many expressions of and around gender variance in India. Any usage of these terms in this volume is therefore not without qualifications.

2 This volume is based on research into the archives of some of the earliest queer support forums in eastern India, literature review and in-depth interviews (face-to-face, through Facebook chat or via email). All interviews were taken with written consent and recorded digitally and/or on paper. Some interviews were entirely in Bengali, Hindi or English, while others were in a mix of these languages. Key expressions in Bengali or Hindi have been retained, but the rest of the conversations in these languages have been translated into English.

in eastern India or elsewhere in the country in the late 1980s or early 1990s. Academic and media discourse have often analysed an amalgam of reasons such as economic liberalization set in motion in the 1990s, a turn towards greater individualism in society, emergence of the HIV epidemic, the attendant 'coming out' of sex and sexuality from the 'cultural closet' into mass media and living rooms, as well as the inflow of large-scale donor funds to facilitate a response to the HIV epidemic (Das and Dhall 2013; Dasgupta and Dhall 2017).

The influences of the feminist movements (both in the West and in India) and the queer movements in the Anglosphere in shaping ideas and identities around sexual orientation and gender identity in India have also been documented. These narratives often show how the gradual participation of the Indian diaspora in these movements encouraged similar action at home (ABVA 1991; Joseph and Dhall 2000). Yet, not all the motivations behind the emergence of queer movements in India had a 'foreign hand'; nor were they only born out of the 'liberalizing' waves of the 1990s. For one, queerness itself is far from a 'Western import'—as is elaborately argued in important works such as Ruth Vanita and Saleem Kidwai's *Same-Sex Love in India: Readings from Literature and History* (2000). Then there are the centuries-old survival efforts of the most visible but also the most criminalized of Indian queer communities—the hijras, who have long lived in guru–chela community structures that, despite being rigidly hierarchical, give them a semblance of security from an exclusionary social environment.

Some writings also show the existence of social networks of different transgender women's communities (or social groups similar to them) in rural and semi-urban areas since the 1990s and even earlier. In West Bengal, for instance, these networks contribute as much as their urban counterparts to queer movements, contrary to the myth that all 'progressive' developments have a foreign-to-Indian or urban-to-rural flow (Dutta 2016). Similarly, oral histories of growing up queer in Kolkata and other literary analyses also reveal the existence of hidden but active queer networks in the city way back in the 1950s and '60s (Partha 1994; Dhall and Karmakar 2015)—even if the queer movements themselves and associated English terms such as 'gay', 'lesbian', 'bisexual' or 'transgender' came much later and still do not have universal resonance with everyone who may be queer in India.

Which of the factors behind queer movements came first would be difficult to establish and can even be an exercise in futility. More so, when trying to assign a definite date or event as a starting point to any social movement brings out the worst in terms of the 'me-first syndrome' on social media. What is important is that a variety of developments led to what came to be the Indian queer movement, or, rather, movements—with many different strands marked by gender identity, sexual orientation, geographical location, class, education, and even caste and race.

At a personal level, there were a number of occasions when it proved challenging to explain the nature of my work or my engagement in trying to set up a queer support forum or publish a queer-themed journal. It was difficult for family and friends—to whom I was out as gay—to fathom these activities as part of a social movement. But however nebulous and hidden, it was a movement in as much as it compelled people to think differently and afresh about sex, gender and sexuality.

Within this context, what has not been talked about enough are the various forms of community mobilization that were deployed in some of the earliest years of the queer movements in India (in this case eastern India), and rarer still has been an analysis of how such mobilization impacted the lives of queer people and their allies in the long run. So the questions here are: How do things appear in retrospect more than 25 years into the queer movements of eastern India? Where or in what state are the people reached out to in the 1990s and later? What bearing do the activisms of the 1990s and early 2000s have on the lives of those individuals today?

Why Have a Queer Movement at All, Let Alone Talk about It?

It is not unbelievable that there still are people who ask why there has to be a women's rights movement or an anti-caste movement. These could be people privileged in various ways and incapable of feeling the pinch, or individuals who have perhaps imbibed and completely normalized the inequalities bestowed on them. For queer movements, establishing a human rights dimension to having a non-normative sexuality and/or gender identity requires crossing equally difficult hurdles. First reactions could be 'But it's something unnatural!' or 'But it's all about *masti* [fun]' or 'Why talk about it, just do it on the side (of marriage and having children)' or even 'How could it be possible?'

In India, there has always been a multiplicity of challenges. One of these has been to counter the argument that diversity around gender and sexuality (more so the latter) is alien to Indian cultures. Then there are the challenges common to queer movements anywhere: to drive home how such diversity attracts invisibilization, oppression, extreme violence, even crim- inalization and therefore deprivation, and also why these social reactions are completely unjustified on grounds of facts and logic in history, art, literature, medicine, health, law, biology or spirituality (Bhugra et al. 2016). The movements have also attempted appealing to the emotions and abstractions of love, affection and trust. They have tried to emphasize that queer rights are not about special rights though they could be about specific needs, just like those of women, young people, the aged, persons with disabilities, or those marginalized on the basis of caste or race. More recently, the emphasis has been to point out the obvious and yet crucial fact that all sections of society over- lap, and that queer people are part of the same social fold rather than a distinct group that can be bundled away out of sight.

The stories within this story may connect a little with all these arguments, some more than the others. But otherwise this volume is not a conscious effort to justify queer movements or the existence of queer people. To borrow from and modify a popular queer movement slogan: 'We're queer; we're here, there and everywhere!'

Placing Myself in the Story

Placing myself in this narrative has been the toughest part— the fact that I have 'lived many of the stories' included in the larger story can be both an advantage and a cause for tension. So, how does one authentically convey the stories and emotions expressed by an interviewee? What if the stories contradict one's experience? In some of the interviews I conducted, I found myself feeling defensive about what the interviewees had to say, especially when they pointed out 'failures' in the queer movement's pathways, or in the way the queer support forums I was associated with as a member and activist functioned in the 1990s or early 2000s. I felt implicated in these 'failures' even when the criticism was not directed at me, or at least not at me alone.

Eventually, the act of writing the story itself helped me make at least partial peace with these feelings. Criticism can be based on incomplete information, but this does not make it unjustified when one realizes that neither the critic nor the objects of their criticism have the whole picture in their head. The criticism then is about failure of communication, which, when I look back, was not uncommon among queer activists and within larger queer social circles. For example, the passion of someone who organized a meeting often sat uneasy with the reluctance of someone unwilling, unable or hesitant to attend, and it did not help if both parties failed to talk it out.

A second realization has been that whatever the failures (or successes) were, if the interviewee still remembers and talks about them to one's face, then such a process should be welcomed. Not only is it a sign that the interviewee actually cares about what one was attempting to do, even if a decade or two ago, it is also invaluable feedback for one's current and future work. This story is in many ways an introspection of work I was part of over the years. Whether it will bring about an emotional closure of sorts is an open question.

* * *

It is strange that even nearly 27 years ago, the act of writing would help me overcome personal disappointments—especially romantic heartbreaks. Rejection in love would so easily be overcome by the next lot of letters from people writing in for information, support, friendship, or to find sexual and romantic partners. Reading their stories and getting engrossed in responding to them acted like a balm for a bruised heart. And now, at the time of writing this book, I am in a three-year-old relationship that has its own set of promises and uncertainties. When it becomes difficult to grapple with the question of whether things will be different this time, writing this narrative acts as a suitable counter to negative thoughts.

The letters in question were mainly addressed to a queer support group that five gay and bisexual men, including me, founded in August 1993 in Kolkata: Counsel Club, one of the earliest forums of its kind in India which existed till 2002. There were two other queer individuals who were closely involved with the formation of the group—both married men who chose to remain anonymous. Many letters were also addressed to *Pravartak* [promoter of a cause],[3] a queer-themed multilingual newsletter. I published the first three issues of *Pravartak* in late 1991 and early 1992 in an individual capacity. At this stage *Pravartak* was entirely in English. After a gap it was revived by Counsel Club as its house journal in 1993, this time with the addition of Bengali and occasional Hindi content (the journal continued till 2000, usually with two issues published each year). Another set of letters were from friends and pen pals, mostly 1989–90 onwards, and many of them were

---

3 It was renamed *Naya Pravartak* in 1995.

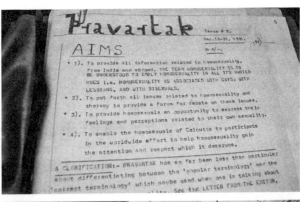

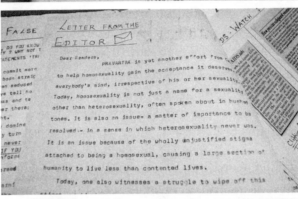

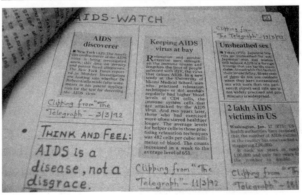

ABOVE. Pages from initial issues of *Pravartak* published independently by the author.

FACING PAGE. First issue of *Pravartak* published as house journal of Counsel Club in 1993.

Pravartak

WASHINGTON
GAY, & BI

History Made By Asian Lesbians

A LOTUS OF ANOTHER COLOR

Rakesh Ratti, editor

An Unfolding of the South Asian Gay and Lesbian...

Friends India

To Promote Amity and Love

Asian Gays Meet I...
Bangkok

The Third International Asian Lesb...
and Gay Conference was held in Bangk...
Thailand from August 24-26, hosted...
the Fraternity for AIDS Cessation
(FACT)...

SHAKTI

BETTER
GAY
THAN
GRUMPY

Dost

BHEDBHAV VIRO...
(AIDS Anti-Discrimination M...
Nov - Dec
1991

NEW GROUP IN CHIN...
"... Times" of London r...
a new group called th...
Group has formed in the...
Public of China to pr...
Liberation. Locat...
province, sou...
...embers

ABOVE. Later issues of *Pravartak* and inside pages of the journal.

FACING PAGE. A Remington portable typewriter used to 'typeset' the initial issues of *Pravartak*.

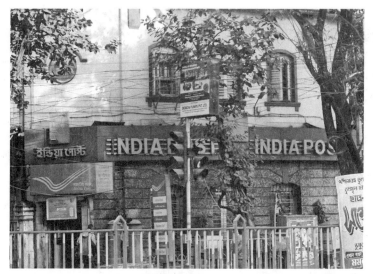

ABOVE. Ballygunge Post Office in South Kolkata, where Counsel Club maintained a post bag. *Photograph by Prosenjit Pal.*

BELOW. Letter from the post office granting request for the post bag. *Photograph by Prosenjit Pal.*

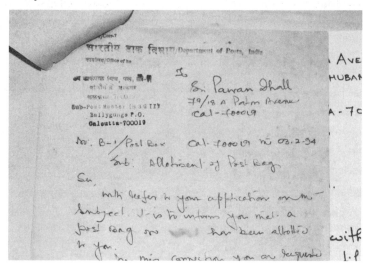

gay or other queer individuals whom I got to know from classified ads in queer journals published in USA, UK and, increasingly, India as well.

When the first lot of queer support groups such as Counsel Club moved towards organized mobilization, one of their biggest challenges was to achieve large-scale outreach. Most of these groups were based in only a handful of urban centres. Beyond word of mouth, or striking lucky in cruising areas (frequented by men interested in men primarily for sexual pick-ups), and opportunities provided by a homosocial environment in familial, friendship and community networks, what worked best was if the groups' post-bag numbers were mentioned in newspaper and magazine articles. This depended a lot on how friendly the journalist or the media house was; but when it worked, it resulted in the groups receiving thousands of letters. This was the pre-Internet era; even acquiring a telephone connection was a tough task.

Counsel Club's Genesis in 1992–93

While I was toying with the idea of a queer support group in Kolkata, having seen an earlier initiative in the city last no longer than a year, as well as similar developments in Delhi in 1992, two of the founder members were referred to me through queer journal *Bombay Dost*, India's first registered queer magazine that started in 1990. I connected with the other four founders through personal ads in other queer journals and a couple of classifieds-only rags (these tabloids were popular for ads from 'broad-minded' people looking for others like them). Of the seven founders, two of us were journalists (I was in my very first job in a business daily, out at home but not at work), a third a college student also freelancing as a journalist, and one chemical engineer, fashion designer, lawyer and entrepreneur apiece. We were in our early 20s to mid 30s. Fellow journalist Raj helped me concretize the idea of a support group over a chat on 15 August 1993, which became the group's foundation day. Three others gave their buy-in during a meeting held soon after, while the other two committed their support from behind the scenes. Since the main purpose of the group was to befriend and counsel each other, the name Counsel Club caught on. I had brought out the first three issues of *Pravartak* independently in 1991–92, and it was Raj's brainwave that we revive it as the house journal of Counsel Club. I now meet only one of the seven founders off and on, though four of us still live in Kolkata.

The letters received by Counsel Club formed a rich repository of not only the lives of lonely, isolated or confused queer individuals but also a society struggling to come to terms with its desires, fears and aspirations. All encapsulated in yellow envelopes, inland forms, open postcards and aerogrammes— from all over West Bengal, nearly all corners of India, and also abroad. In terms of the letters' language, Bengali and English dominated, with a sprinkling of Hindi and occasional Gujarati.

The demographics ranged from youth in their late teens and early 20s to individuals in their 40s and 50s, presumably most of them from the middle classes and with literacy levels that at times allowed for fairly evocative articulations. Men, or, more accurately, persons assigned male at birth, constituted a vast

FACING PAGE AND OVERLEAF. Letters from the Counsel Club archives maintained by Varta Trust.

Dear Pawan,
I had received your
time back - but I am
not- reply early, par
day long, then at
shop to attend hours c
ng or I a letter was so
exercise. I was hope

Dear Sir,
    I am a 26 years old, fair and hand...
from Guwahati, Assam and a postgradua...
...dent. Recently, from the newsletter "...
...", I have come to know about your cl...
...e newsletter "PRAVARTAK". I have alre...
...moneyorder for a sample copy of "PRA...

    Sir, I started sensing my homose...
...t the age of 11. Though, till now, I...
...had sex with anybody, I feel intense...
...do it when I see young handsome guys...
I feel very lonely and dessected an...
...suffering from mental depression. ...
help me. If you have any informati...
...en from Guwahati, please giv...

(১) শ্রী সুশান্ত
(সদস্য, কার্যকরী সভা)

২২/৫/৯৫

... তার কাছে চিঠি দিলাম। তার
Response নেই। ... তার সেক্রেটারি
রুম নম্বর নং। ... আমি Reply Envelope
পাঠাই - বি, দ্বিতীয়ত, তার বিভাগের কর্মকর্তা...

... হইবার উত্তর পাই। আমি তার
চিঠি পাবার পর জানিয়েছিলাম, তার ঠিকানা
ছিল শাখা হতে চিঠি। তার চিঠিতে কোন
ঠিকানা ছিল না। তোমার বিষয়ে তার ...
... ? আমি তোমার, তোমার ...

Dear Pawan,

22.12.90

आपका पत्र मिला। आप कैसे हैं? आप ...
... मिला। आप की ... ... New Perspective
...

29.12.90

Pav/प्रिय मित्र,
...

Dear ব্রত,

Calcutta
June 17, 1938

Pawan -এর সাথে আমার শেষ সাক্ষাৎ
meeting -এ হবার কথা ... । Pawan -এর সাথে
... এই letter টা তে দিলাম
... । ২২ তারিখ ... ...
... — সেই মিটিং-এ ... ... ।
... English term -এ appropriate ...
... । ... চিঠির appropri...
... modify করে দিই। ... ...
... চিঠির কোন; এই সব সুযোগ ...
... আমার । বিশেষ আমার ২৫ তারিখ...

majority of the letter writers. In terms of occupation, they included college and university students, teachers, doctors, lawyers, journalists, artists, researchers and homemakers (among just a few examples). Many letters were sent in by NGOs, media houses, bookstores and queer groups or journals from other countries looking to establish links with their Indian counterparts or write about the Indian queer scenario.

From brief and hesitating inquiries about Counsel Club and *Pravartak*, animated queries about access to sexual partners and spaces for having sex, to personal outpourings of loneliness, grief, oppression, unhappy marriages, sexual experiences and love stories—these letters were a microcosm of an India that was sexually active, liberal, inquisitive, orthodox and repressed, all at the same time. In some cases, it was not clear what the letter writer was looking for, possibly because of incomplete comprehension about what Counsel Club and *Pravartak* stood for.

As fate and my passion for documentation would have it, I still have 2,500 to 3,000 of Counsel Club and *Pravartak*'s letters,[4] greeting cards, some emails from the early Videsh Sanchar Nigam Limited era, photographs (or their negatives) of Counsel Club's activities, copies of *Pravartak*, and other material as part of an informal archive maintained by Varta Trust, Kolkata—an NGO that I co-founded in 2012 to publish, research and advocate on gender and sexuality issues, and in some ways to carry forward the work of Counsel Club and *Pravartak*.

* * *

---

4 My personal letters not included.

In September 1996, a little more than two years since obtaining *Pravartak* and Counsel Club's contact through two articles in the *Statesman* newspaper (Sharma 1994; Phukan 1994), lovers Meenakshi and Jyoti (names changed) wrote in saying that they needed immediate help. Both were around 22, MA students in the same institution in Kolkata, and were facing the inevitable and urgent pressure from their 'very conservative' families to get married. They were resolute that marriage in the conventional sense was not an option, but if they could not be together, then suicide would be *the* option.

Counsel Club was in its third year then, and issues such as marriage pressure, people running away from home and suicide attempts (including successful ones) by queer people were not alien to us. But there was something compelling about this letter, written in blue fountain-pen ink on ruled notebook paper, in grammatically imperfect yet clear English. The writers seemed unpretentious but quietly determined. Besides, this was the first request of its kind received from women, and the Counsel Club core group, which we often called 'the group that did most of the work most of the time' (Sanjay 1997–98), was gripped with a sense of new urgency.

By this time, only two of Counsel Club's founders (including me) were still actively engaged in the group, and the composition of the core group had evolved in terms of numbers, gender, class, language, religion and other social parameters. In the initial years, most of the core-group members had been from middle- or upper-middle-class backgrounds and somewhat more comfortable in English (even if equally fluent in Bengali and Hindi). But one of the newest members, Rafiquel Haque

ALTERNATE SEXUALITY

Lesbians in India, a large invisible minority, are now determined to uncover truths from the past and find a present

Love
Ute
come walk w
tell me some
stories
I am tired of
mine
I will listen
I am unloa
overload
and listen
walk.
— — Zari

PAUL DAVIES on how the mind works 2 ■ The Whi
from Yale 4 ■ **FIFA's** new laws mean little

Dowjah aka Ranjan, brought in a fresh perspective. His experiences as a queer person from a lower-middle-class background were different in many ways, and he pushed for an approach in Counsel Club's activities that would factor in the concerns of queer people from less privileged circumstances. He also had a better grasp of Bengali and brought in greater use of the language in the group's communication and in *Pravartak*'s content. He had a street smartness that gave him a hands-on flair for crisis management.

I sent off an immediate reply to Meenakshi and Jyoti asking to arrange a meeting, and Ranjan joined me in coordinating support for the two women. We met for the first time at South Pole, an old-time, now closed eatery in the crowded Gariahat area of Kolkata. The eatery was at a 'safe' distance from the two women's homes and college, and busy enough to provide a degree of anonymity as we plotted their next move. Within weeks, Meenakshi and Jyoti were to leave their homes for Delhi, Ranjan playing the most crucial role in helping them do so.

The couple's flight turned out to be no less than a cross-country Great Escape. We sought legal advice from Stree Sangam (now LABIA), a queer women's support group in Mumbai, and Swayam, an NGO working with women facing domestic violence in Kolkata. We gained crucial knowledge about what needs to be done if an individual, even if adult, plans to leave home on their own accord in India. The to-do checklist seemed to include equal parts socially required items and legally required ones— perhaps because the escapees were women, and even more so

FACING PAGE. Issue of the *Statesman* newspaper supplement that included articles carrying Counsel Club's contact through which Meenakshi and Jyoti wrote in.

women in love with each other. Both women were advised to send letters by registered post to their respective local police stations informing them that they were leaving home. They had to attach evidence of their adulthood and emphasize the fact that they were leaving on their own accord. A list of items they were taking with them had to be attached as well, with specific mention of jewellery and its ownership. The emphasis was on anticipating 'moral guardianship' by the police (on behalf of the families), not just against the escapees but also against people enabling their escape.

In Delhi, the destination point, it was a network of queer activists, allies and a pioneering women's rights group that provided the couple initial shelter and, subsequently, livelihood opportunities as well as help in finding rented accommodation. Without their assurances, Meenakshi and Jyoti may not have been able to make the move. Similarly, in Kolkata, queer community members risked family objections and provided the couple temporary but crucial shelter till they boarded the train. Looking back, this was a journey unaided by the technology of mobile phones and debit cards—or, should I say, unhampered by their tell-tale digital footprints? Even the railway tickets were booked 'offline', hurriedly, in a sweaty queue—based on the best window of opportunity for the two women to leave home.

Both women knew their respective families would have figured out that they had run away together. Their friendship since first year of graduation studies in 1992 was well known both in the college, where they were classmates, and in each other's homes. Jyoti was already unpopular in Meenakshi's house, one reason possibly being she had unconventional looks 'for a woman'. They phoned back from Delhi (without revealing their location) and asked their families not to come after them. Fortunately, their families agreed, perhaps realizing the legal futility of the process. Meenakshi kept her family informed about her well-being through letters posted from different cities for about a year before revealing her location; Jyoti never wrote to her family.

EARLY ALLIES OF QUEER MOVEMENTS IN EASTERN INDIA

Veena Lakhumalani and Dr Sujit Ghosh

Veena Lakhumalani is now retired but still engages in consultancies on child protection, human rights and education. She is based in Pune, Maharashtra, and helps NGOs access funds from the corporate sector and international donors. When she came in touch with Counsel Club in 1994, she was with the British Council Division in Kolkata, leading its health and social development unit and managing large projects on HIV, disability and human rights. Along with HIV co-trainer Dr Sujit Ghosh, a psychiatrist and sexual-health expert, she was introduced to Counsel Club by group member Debanuj Dasgupta, who first met them in context of his sociology course in Presidency College. Both readily agreed to act as mentors to the group and, up till the late 1990s, helped shape many of the group's values, skills and knowledge around sexual health and human rights. In the course of my research for this volume, I did not get an opportunity to speak to Sujit (now living in the UK) but had a long nostalgic chat with Veena in early September 2017 during one of her visits to Kolkata.

In the mid 1990s, the British Council established the West Bengal Sexual Health Project (WBSHP), one of the earliest government–civil society collaborative responses to the HIV epidemic in India. Both

Veena and Sujit were among the key trainers engaged with the project. Veena spoke about the genesis of WBSHP, the excitement around it among community groups and in the media, and how her involvement in the project was something she had never imagined as part of her career. While she was already familiar with the concerns of injecting drug users in Kolkata through a campaign run in collaboration with ad agency Thoughtshop Communications, this project led her to interact with sex workers and eventually gay men and other queer people. Counsel Club too became part of the project through her and Sujit's efforts in making the initiative more inclusive.

As Veena developed links with the queer communities, she found herself supporting them at several levels. The sexual-health training workshops under WBSHP provided her opportunities to address myths around homosexuality. When a young gay friend was bashed up by a ruffian posing as a police official, she guided the victim to file an FIR with the police. She personally followed up the matter with the police and reported it to officials at the highest level in the West Bengal government. She made every effort that the state government at least acknowledged the existence of queer people in Kolkata and Bengal.

On a humorous note, she talked about how her single-woman status, combined with her work with sex workers and queer people, raised many eyebrows and led to countless speculations. For example: 'We had a consultant on one of our projects who was gay, very obviously gay. He was extremely nice and we became very good friends. In those days when we couldn't get Western classical music here, he had the most amazing collection of LP records. So I used to go to his house and listen to music. Everybody knew he was gay, but we were often seen going out for meals together. And he wanted to learn Indian cooking. So Sunday mornings, I would go and sit with him for a while, with beautiful music playing in the background, and I would be teaching him recipes. And people were confused. Is he gay or not gay? Why is Veena with him?' (*More on the conversation with Veena in later pages.*)

Before I met Meenakshi for the interview for this volume, I met her briefly in 2014, nearly 17 years since I last saw her in Delhi. This was at a public event in Kolkata on engaging men in the struggle for gender equity, co-organized by the NGO Meenakshi then worked for (and still does). In a quick conversation, she informed me that she was back in Kolkata, had separated from Jyoti about four years ago, and was now married to a man who was also part of her and Jyoti's friend circle from back in college. She was also mother to a two-year-old child. Some people at work knew about her past, but by and large she preferred being discreet about it.

We promised to catch up soon, curious as I was about the huge upheavals Meenakshi seemed to have undergone over the years. But it was not until the interview for this volume, in November 2017, that we sat together over coffee, not once but thrice, for a prolonged and emotional sharing (part of it off the record) of the journeys of our lives over two decades. In fact, I would not have had spent as much time during all my meetings with Meenakshi and Jyoti back in 1996–97 in Kolkata and Delhi.[5]

---

5 A similar interview was not attempted with Jyoti because it appeared from Meenakshi's interview that Jyoti would prefer not to be contacted. Jyoti had

Meenakshi began hesitatingly, but gradually got into the flow, and seemed relieved to be able to talk freely about the trajectory of her life, many elements of which she had kept to herself for a long time: 'In Delhi, it was a very different world. Because I was coming from a very protected, very conservative, middle-class family from Calcutta, and going there, it was like starting life from scratch, and having very, very few resources . . . it was a culture shock, because Calcutta's community feeling, living in a *para* [neighbourhood], we grew up with that feeling. But in Delhi, my god, people were so aggressive, everywhere, on roads, public transport. Workplace was the only place where we used to feel that there are other people also who'd listen to what we had to say.'

However, Meenakshi and Jyoti proved to be quick learners. Within three months of their arrival in Delhi, they got jobs with a women's rights group. Their post-graduation studies in Hindi literature proved useful. Meenakshi got busy with contributing extensively to the NGO's magazine in Hindi and its documentation centre.

'While working there, I explored what I wanted to do in life. It felt as if I was in the right place and this was the kind of work I always wanted to do. I got exposed to women's issues, I had a lot of my own questions with gender, and I felt that I was a born feminist, without knowing the word "feminist"! I heard the word for the first time only after going to Delhi. Here in

---

also not maintained contact with many of our common friends and tracing her independently of Meenakshi would have required time beyond what was available. Nevertheless, exploring a separate conversation with Jyoti remains a possibility sometime in future.

Kolkata, as part of our literature studies, we were aware about women's issues [*mahilaavaad*], but I heard about feminism [*naarivaad*] for the first time in Delhi . . . I could associate very well with the whole world of working on rights.' Explaining the shift in her understanding from literary to political, Meenakshi said that while in Kolkata she had read pioneers like Hindi fiction writer Shivani and sociopolitical activist Mahasweta Devi. But the work experience in Delhi helped her learn about the history of revolutions behind feminism and develop a stronger political sense on women's issues.

She was frank about why she did not give deeper thought to women's issues while in Kolkata. Studying Hindi literature was enjoyable but more a compulsion for the sake of marks. It was not even her first choice. She ended up pursuing it rather than psychology because the only colleges offering psychology courses then were co-educational, which was not agreeable to her parents. The escape to Delhi, therefore, was about multiple freedoms!

Meenakshi went on to do a second post-graduation, this time in human rights, through a distance-learning course. 'I felt it'd be good for my work and career, and it was also very interesting to read about laws, and really going beyond women's rights to looking at the different people's rights, especially marginalized people's rights.' Meenakshi also wrote a paper on sexual harassment at the workplace, which was published and became part of the training curriculum of the Indian Institute of Human Rights. 'It was a big achievement for the organization as well as personally for me!' Her excitement was palpable as she talked about the training experience she gained at the

NGO she worked with and credited it with building her professional base. Other successes followed in Meenakshi's career—such as when she became involved in organizing the Seventh National Conference on Women's Movements in India held in Kolkata in 2006, or when she rose to the position of deputy director in her organization.

* * *

As I listened to Meenakshi, I remembered other queer individuals and couples from eastern India who did not have the same fortune and success as Meenakshi and Jyoti. One such couple was Mamata and Monalisa from a village near Cuttack in Odisha. Neighbours in the same village, they had been in a relationship for five years. When Monalisa's father received a transfer order to a different place, she did not want to move. But her family persisted, and perhaps at this point the couple felt all options running out. In late 1998, they attempted a joint suicide, in which Monalisa passed away but Mamata survived.

Apparently, the villagers had taken their relationship to be a close friendship. But the suicide attempt changed things. It attracted extremely negative and salacious media attention, which led to the villagers turning against Mamata. Monalisa's family filed a police complaint against her for 'murdering' their daughter even as she struggled to overcome her own trauma in a nursing home in Cuttack.

The Counsel Club archives have a series of letters (through late 1998 and early 1999) exchanged with two individuals who possibly read media reports on Mamata and Monalisa, and then contacted Counsel Club for help through queer activists in Mumbai. Another letter was from AIDS Bhedbhav Virodhi

Andolan (ABVA), a civil rights group based in Delhi, which

showed that the two women had even filed an affidavit before a court that they wanted to live together. A 'survival strategy' rare by even today's standards, this indicates that their families may have already known about their relationship, and the couple may have anticipated a potentially forced separation.

In February–March 1999, ABVA conducted a fact-finding mission to Cuttack to interact with the two women's families as well as police, media and other individuals. Later they published a report titled *People Like Us*, which documented Mamata and Monalisa's tragic story as well as other similar incidents involving queer individuals. Counsel Club on its part was unable to do much in response; we only had a couple of queer community contacts in Odisha and little wherewithal to act outside Bengal or even Kolkata. Furthermore, at that time the group's leadership itself was in a flux, and this, in my memory, also prevented a meaningful response.

Subsequently, we lost track of Mamata, but this incident remained indelible in our minds. There was some consolation in the fact that the few contacts we had in Odisha proved instrumental in starting tentative community-mobilization efforts in the state in 2000, though it was not until the second half of the 2000s that the queer movement developed a stronger footing in the state. By this time both Counsel Club and *Pravartak* had wound up but newer support forums had come up in eastern India.

Same-sex marriages are not legally recognized in India, but the law does not debar a ritualistic wedding between two women, two men or even a transgender person and their partner (provided the individuals concerned are adults). Such weddings are off and on in the news, and sometimes even have some social sanction. The wedding of policewomen Leela and Urmila in Bhopal in 1987 is often cited as one of the first such marriages documented in contemporary India, though it cost them their jobs on grounds of dereliction of duties. Queer support groups and helplines often have to deal with queries around same-sex marriage, and they do not tire of explaining the difference between social and legal recognition of same-sex marriages. What they also explain is that Indian law does not disallow two adults, irrespective of gender, from living together. But social oppression (including moral policing by those in uniform) against any kind of divergence from so-called norms continues to have a crippling stranglehold on the lives of queer people in India, irrespective of their age.

A version of Mamata and Monalisa's story was played out in February 2011 near Nandigram in West Bengal when cousins Swapna and Sucheta declared their love for each other in a suicide note, consumed poison in a paddy field and killed themselves. They could see no way out against the opposition of their families and village elders. According to a news report in the *Indian Express* (Dasgupta 2011) and a fact-finding mission conducted by Sappho for Equality, a Kolkata-based support forum for lesbian, bisexual women and transgender men,[6] their

---

6 Sappho for Equality (www.sapphokolkata.in) works for the rights of sexually marginalized women and transgender men in eastern India, and is a registered body started in 2003. It works parallel to Sappho, which is an informal support group exclusively for lesbians, bisexual women and transgender men (LBT people) started in 1999. Sappho for Equality has a larger membership framework consisting of both LBT individuals and their allies.

families even refused to perform their last rites, leaving their bodies unclaimed in the morgue.

Conclusions based on just a handful of incidents may be misplaced, and it is not as if all queer people living in urban areas face less stigma than their rural counterparts, or that support for queer people in rural areas is completely absent. However, unlike Meenakshi and Jyoti, the other people mentioned were not located in an urban centre like Kolkata where, if nothing else, queer affirmation is more visible and support systems easier to access. What was possible for Meenakshi and Jyoti in 1996 was not so for others even many years later. Preventing violence across a wider geographical canvas remains a daunting task for queer support groups, even as queer movements have become more resourceful over the years.

EARLY ALLIES OF QUEER MOVEMENTS IN EASTERN INDIA

Veena Lakhumalani on Her Interactions with Queer Support Group Sappho in Its Earliest Stages

'When I met them [in 1999] their core group was eight ladies, and then for the first time I heard in some ways it's far more difficult for women than for the men. Because women's lives are much more proscribed, and a woman has to get married, she must have children, there are expectations of the family. A young man can get away with anything because he's a guy—what do you expect?

'When I heard the horror stories of how in the case of two [female] couples their own parents reported them to the police and used Section 377 of the Indian Penal Code to put their own children in jail—this for me was absolutely not acceptable. So we were going to organize a human rights film and cartoon festival from the British Council's side [in 2000], and I decided to add a day on the rights of gay people [see British Council 2000]. I didn't deliberately say "lesbian" because they were not willing to come out in the open. But we met them a lot and they had no space for their meetings. They met in my house a few times, and then in the British Council. And then when we had the film festival, although they said we will not tell people [about their sexual orientation], somebody made a very provocative statement, which set the whole place on fire. So some of these ladies just got up and spoke up—I don't remember what they said, but it set the scene. Because then a lot of issues came out, and for me this whole programme was about human rights of different communities. I think that was the most successful day!

'Subsequently we organized a film festival only on lesbian issues, and it was a much smaller group. They brought in films and I also brought some. It was a group of about 16 to 20, but it also had representatives from the Jadavpur University School of Women's Studies and Calcutta University, and a couple of researchers and so on. Though I knew people were talking about me because I was unmarried, I was involved in lesbian issues, I must be lesbian, but I didn't bother because once I had launched into it I was determined to do what I could do. Later I also helped them set up a website. But the dramatic thing was how after the film festival their membership shot up from around a dozen to several times more within 10 days to a month, across eastern India, and even Bangladesh and Nepal. And over the years of course one watched them grow and grow and grow!'

The conversation with Meenakshi turned towards more personal issues. Youngest of three siblings, she was very fond of her father and was his favourite as well. 'As I said, I was part of a protective family environment. When I started attending college here in Kolkata—from school to college, it was a big move. In college it was a multicultural environment. Here I made a new friend [Jyoti], someone very special to me. We were in the same class. We started talking about a whole lot of issues, sharing things that we hadn't discussed with others. She was the first person who I could be very comfortable with, about the troubles I was going through at home. She comforted and reassured me that I shouldn't blame myself for whatever was going wrong. This was a big strength.'

Meenakshi felt she grew up a lonely child in spite of the love and affection at home. 'There was a lot going on inside me, and I had no one to share it with. College was where I could unburden myself and Jyoti became very, very special.' Cheering up a bit, she recalled: 'One of the first incidents of the *kuch kuch hota hai* kind[7] actually happened—this is one of those things people talk about that makes you feel that you have really lived it. This was in the first year of college. We both used to come early to college, when nobody would be around. Why, we didn't know then! It just felt good to meet and talk to each other. So one day, as much as I can barely recall, I probably said something about jumping off the window in our class room. Immediately—and this I remember clearly—she said she too

---

7 An expression popularized by the 1998 Hindi romantic drama film *Kuch Kuch Hota Hai*, which implies the heart experiencing a pleasantly unsettling sensation in the presence of a person one is attracted to.

would jump after me. I was aghast that here was someone ready to give their life for me! It was so *filmi* and I was only 18.'

Things began to change for Meenakshi and Jyoti after this—they were drawn to each other; they were always together in class, sometimes spending time in a coffee house near college. They started visiting each other's homes (Jyoti coming over to Meenakshi more often than the other way around) and sharing family matters. Meenakshi's father and extended family members did not quite like Jyoti, wondering why the two spent so much time together. When Meenakshi had a lengthy sickness, they even suspected Jyoti to be responsible for it, based on a traditional healer's remark. The entire episode angered Meenakshi no end, and she did not speak to her father till he apologized.

The two women remained inseparable, with Meenakshi often looking up to her companion: 'Jyoti was the person who taught me to mix with different people. In a way our family was quite liberal—my father was an avid reader, and had a socialist bent of mind. But there was also this issue of caste. There was a feeling of caste superiority in my family. Even before moving to Delhi or coming to know of any organization, Jyoti was the person who taught me to question all this, and to do very basic things like sharing food with others. She taught me to trust others. That I think eventually became the reason I could leave my parents and my house.'

While Meenakshi and Jyoti were certain they wanted to be together, they were also wondering how to make it happen. For Meenakshi, the marriage pressure was getting stronger by the day, while Jyoti had to contend with three domineering elder brothers, with little support from her widowed mother. There were financial imponderables of life away from home. Their university studies were headed for completion and they did not have any job prospects that would have helped stave off the marriage pressure for a while. At this point, they happened to visit a common friend who too was in a relationship with another woman but had given in to the pressure to get married. Her situation further unnerved Meenakshi and Jyoti and they were almost sure that a joint suicide would be the only way out.

Remembering the evening they met the common friend (now widowed and settled in Chennai), Meenakshi said: 'It suddenly started raining heavily with thunder and storm. So we postponed it. We thought not today, it's not going to work because already we are late and then listening to her story, what she was going through . . . then we both came back. And it's a miracle! Sometimes I don't believe what happened to me, it was like something supernatural or divine. After a few days I was clearing up my cupboard, and discovered, in the newspaper that had been used to line the shelf below my books, the article in the *Statesman* published in 1994—and this I'm talking about '96, after two years. And I read the article because there was a picture of two women together and other pictures [from activist-researcher Giti Thadani's collection—she was then looking into depiction of love between women in Indian mythology]. Then there were a few addresses, including that of *Pravartak*. I was thrilled after reading that article! And I was like *arrey teri to, hum bhi to aisay* feel *karte hain* [oh god, we feel just like this]— so it's not something odd, or a problem or disease! It's nothing but human desire—we didn't understand the language or the politics, we just knew that we were two people who loved each other and wanted to be together. That was the first realization that what we wanted could be possible.'

Meenakshi had to wait all of the weekend before she could share the article with Jyoti in college. They both read the article 'with a dictionary' to grasp numerous unfamiliar terms and, given their 'desperation', eventually agreed that they had nothing to lose in writing to *Pravartak*. Their common friend played a major role as they used the common friend's postal address for communication with *Pravartak*.

Meenakshi remembered sharing many of the doubts crowding their minds with Ranjan and me in our first meeting. They were fearful about moving to Delhi, which was, even at that time, seen as a 'criminal city'. There was little time to go through a counselling process to consider the pros and cons of a move to the Indian capital. Meenakshi was more shaky and uncertain, but Jyoti was decisive. Given her much more oppressive family circumstances, she was clear that a move had to be made when there was a fighting chance, and that their move had to be timed together. Eventually, with assurances from people in both Kolkata and Delhi, and an understanding that if all failed they could still end their lives together, Meenakshi and Jyoti took what was nothing short of a great leap of faith for the sake of their relationship.

* * *

While in Meenakshi and Jyoti's case there was a concrete response that could be worked out by Counsel Club and other queer support groups and activists, there was precious little that was possible when Ryan (name changed) wrote in from Shillong, Meghalaya, in August 1999 seeking help for a 'sex change'. In the second year of their BA course, Ryan read about Counsel Club in an article on 'women in love' in *Sunday* magazine in May 1998 (Dhamija 1998): 'I read inside and was very happy to see that there were helpline [sic] addresses. I am also one of them. Thou [sic], I was born as a girl but my behaviour and attitude are not of a girl. I am different from what a girl is. I don't like at all to be a girl. I like to be a boy. I don't also like to wear girl's stuff. I do wear boy's stuff.'

Going on to describe how their troubles had set them back in their studies, Ryan's letter conveyed an utter sense of helplessness: 'For having this kind of life there is so much pain . . . There have been so much difficulties with this female body within me [sic], sometimes I could feel the pain and all I could do is to only cry to myself.'

Ryan's family provided little support: 'My family does not understand, when I explain about how my life is. Instead, they say that it is better to talk to a doctor who knows about this, but they never do . . . now I stop telling them because I get no help from them. I just kept it to myself.' It is at this point that Ryan says they came to know about Counsel Club and their hopes were kindled: 'I thought to myself that there is some hope for my life. Please understand and help me sir / madame. All I want is to go for sex-change [sic]. I have seen and read in other magazine that many have undergone sex operation. You are my only hope.'

The archival records show that I wrote two letters in response, the first a quick one to reassure Ryan within three days of the letter being received on 7 September 1999 (this was just before a trip to Asansol and Durgapur for Counsel Club's work). The second letter was lengthier and written after consultation with other members of the Counsel Club letter-writing team and collection of relevant information. But a copy of the second response shows that there was not much concrete support that we could offer.

All I could write was a word of reassurance that Ryan was not alone in their predicament, and that we should try and locate a counsellor who would help Ryan take a considered and well-informed decision on undergoing a 'sex-change operation'. I wanted Ryan to be aware of the 'emotional, medical, social, financial and legal issues' involved. I sought Ryan's permission to share excerpts from their letter (keeping their identity confidential) with counsellors in Kolkata and to spread the word through the Internet in order to locate support groups that could have helped Ryan better than Counsel Club. I also encouraged Ryan to write about their interests and career plans in the hope of continuing our conversation and exploring other ways of assisting them.

Ryan did not write back, and I remember the nagging worry we used to feel while responding to people at their residential addresses. What if their letter was opened by someone else and they got into trouble for having contacted a group such as ours? I made discreet enquiries with friends in Shillong, but I could not trace Ryan for an interview after these many years. Ironically, when I read my response today, I can think of several options to suggest to Ryan that did not exist then—Syrngiew, a queer women's support forum in Shillong itself; Xukia, another queer support group two hours away by road in Guwahati;

Sappho, which had just about started in Kolkata (in June 1999); as well as health- and legal-aid service providers in Meghalaya and neighbouring states. All of these are outcomes of queer activism that can be traced to the 1990s, initially in West Bengal and Manipur, and eventually, in the late 2000s, in the larger region of North-East India.

In their letter Ryan said they felt like a boy. Today, when queer identities and lexicon have become more diverse and visible, Ryan may have identified as 'transgender', 'transgender boy', 'trans man' or even 'trans masculine'. But in their letter they never once mentioned any of these terms. Perhaps being able to put a more specific 'name' to their situation could have lessened their pain to some extent. At the same time, it would have been Ryan's choice how to identify or whether to identify with any term at all. And I would not have said today what I did in my letter then—trying to correct a 'mistake' in Ryan's perceptions, that the article in *Sunday* was on lesbians and bisexual women, while they 'might be a transsexual person'.

EARLY ALLIES OF QUEER MOVEMENTS IN EASTERN INDIA

Dr Sherry Joseph

Sherry first wrote to Counsel Club in 1995 while pursuing a PhD in social work at Delhi University, with a focus on queer issues. His initial letters caused considerable excitement in the group because somebody associated with a major university had written to us, which meant we were going places! In 1996, he shifted to Visva-Bharati University in Santiniketan to teach social work. What followed was a long association that was rewarding for both Sherry and Counsel Club at several levels—research, knowledge and skills, activism and bonds of friendship that included his wife Linu, an advocate, and their first child Annette, now all grown up and in Christ University in Bangalore.

Sherry was among a growing tribe of academics writing on queer issues in those years. Apart from having his articles on such topics published in the *Economic & Political Weekly*, he also authored a book titled *Social Work Practice and Men Who Have Sex with Men* (2005). It was based extensively on Sherry's interaction with Counsel Club and other queer groups or networks in Kolkata in the 1990s, though the book itself was published in 2005. My first-ever CV entry on an academic publication was in collaboration with Sherry—we contributed an article 'No Silence Please, We're Indians! Les-Bi-Gay Voices from India' to 'Different Rainbows', an anthology of queer activist writings from developing countries (Joseph and Dhall 2000).

Sherry left Visva-Bharati University around 2002 for a job with Catholic Bishops Conference of India, which was then engaged in one of the largest HIV care, support and treatment programmes in collaboration with National AIDS Control Organisation. Subsequently, after a stint with the Futures Group in Delhi, he shifted abroad, continuing to work on HIV projects—first with the UNAIDS Technical Support Facility for South Asia in Nepal, and then the United Nations Development Programme in Sudan. That was where Sherry had returned from, not long before I met him at his home in Ernakulam in December 2017. There was much to reminisce over Sherry's homemade wine. This was an apt way to reconnect after we last met in 2007, when Sherry visited Kolkata from Delhi for work and helped me discover the efficacy of brandy with warm water to soothe a sore throat.

Speaking about his association with Counsel Club, Sherry said:

'The best part I remember—I was telling Allen also [Sherry's second child]—that it was my *adda* when I used to go to Calcutta [from Santiniketan], your house used to be like an *adda*. I still remember the hospitality that you and your mom provided. There were the group meetings in the evenings, visits to parks, our conversations. That was a very good phase of life . . . When Annette was born in 1997, I was in a conference on queer issues in Bombay, presenting a paper on human rights. I was there when I got a call that Linu has been hospitalized, her labour pains have come. I had no time to get train tickets and rush home! Then Annette was there when Counsel Club celebrated its fifth birthday—I remember Linu and her cutting the cake.' (Counsel Club archives have a photograph of the occasion celebrated in 1998 at George Bhawan in central Kolkata, venue of the group's fortnightly meetings from mid 1997 till early 2002.)

In a curious turn of events, Annette found her father's book (*Social Work Practice*) stocked in her university library in 2016. When she excitedly reported this to Sherry, he did a Google search and was surprised to find that the book had become an important reference for many other studies and publications. (*More on the conversation with Sherry on his research work in later pages.*)

The distinction between 'lesbian' or 'gay' and 'transgender' or 'transsexual' is crucial. The first two signify a person's sexual attraction (which may be towards men, women, both, someone androgynous or no one at all) while the next two indicate what the person feels about their gender (which may be male, female, both, neither or something else). Similarly, a distinction is often made between 'transgender' and 'transsexual'. In general, 'transgender' stands for a person whose own sense of gender is not aligned with the sex (and gender) assigned to them at birth, and may even transcend the gender binary of male/female, say, as in the expression 'third gender' (Pattojoshi et al. 2017). The term 'transsexual', now losing currency, signifies transgender persons who undergo (or want to undergo) gender-reaffirmation procedures to align their bodies with their sense of gender identity. But I have also experienced the pitfalls of activist enthusiasm to get the terms right at the expense of the priorities of the person across me. Many of us have come around to believe (through innumerable day-to-day interactions, research and training) that there is no one way to be man, woman, gay, lesbian, transgender, transsexual, Hindu, Muslim, Indian or anything else. Thus it should not have been my place to 'correct' Ryan if they somehow felt kinship with the women in love portrayed in the magazine.

Meenakshi and Jyoti too did not quite self-identify as lesbians in their first letter: 'We the two students of MA [want] to live together. In your words we are lesbian . . .' But they were clear about who they desired and what they wanted ahead in their lives. Again, in retrospect, queer activism in the early 1990s was only just beginning to grapple with the lexicon. Counsel Club's archival records show that till the late 1990s, 'transsexual' was more commonly in use than 'transgender', which then gradually gained popularity as an umbrella expression for gender non-conformance. In essence, the queer movement was (and still is) about continuously exploring what words express one's feelings most accurately.

* * *

The search for better self-expression cannot, by or in itself, be faulted. If the personal is political and means to rightful self-assertion, then the politics of identity cannot be silenced. But when it assumes a rigid form, marked with rivalries of different sorts, the outcomes may not be happy. Aparna was in her early 20s when she contacted Counsel Club nearly 18 years ago after reading an article in the Bengali daily *Anandabazar Patrika* (Basu 1999).[8] On 14 December 2017, when we meet after a media conference at the Kolkata Press Club, she speaks of the dangers posed by a new central legislation in the making on transgender rights.

This proposed legislation is the Transgender Persons (Protection of Rights) Bill, 2016, which, after several community consultations since August 2016, is supposed to have facilitated the implementation of a ground-breaking verdict from the Supreme Court of India on transgender identities and citizenship rights declared on 15 April 2014 in the case of *National Legal Services Authority (NALSA) v. Union of India and Others*. Instead, the bill has attracted vehement criticism and public protests by transgender communities and allies across India (Banerjie 2017; Semmalar 2017). A simple reading of the bill shows that it waters down the progressive intent and directions of the apex court's verdict on almost all fronts: in defining 'transgender' it conflates the concept with 'intersex';[9] instead

---

8 Aparna's letter was not answered by me, and it is not part of the Counsel Club archival records maintained by Varta Trust (portions of Counsel Club's records would be with other members of the erstwhile support group).

9 According to the United Nations for LGBT Equality, intersex persons are born with sex characteristics (including one or more of the following: genitals,

of honouring the right to self-identify one's gender, it talks about certification of gender by district screening committees; it does not acknowledge the specific concerns of transgender men; it pays token attention to anti-discrimination and health-protection measures; and it may well end up criminalizing hijra[10] households or families, the last resort to shelter for many

---

gonads, sex hormones and chromosomal patterns) that are ambiguous in terms of the typical definitions of male or female. Intersex stands for a range of sexual and reproductive anatomical possibilities and not for a fixed 'third' category of biological sex. If this difference from so-called norms is discovered at birth, intersex persons are assigned one or the other sex (and gender) by doctors based on social considerations and surgical interventions. Sometimes the difference may be discovered during adolescence or later, or may never be discovered. Intersex communities strongly argue that the 'medical normalization' or 'correctional surgeries' carried out at birth should be stopped and the person should be allowed to choose whichever gender they are comfortable with once they are legally old enough to decide. A related point is that being intersex and being transgender are two different issues, though they may have an overlap. Some intersex persons may grow up to identify with a gender different from the one assigned to them at birth, and they may consider themselves to be transgender. But that does not make all intersex people transgender. Conversely, transgender people are those whose own sense of gender is not aligned with the sex (and gender) assigned to them at birth. But not all of them are born with a sexual or reproductive anatomy that is ambiguous in terms of being assigned male or female at birth.

10 Hijras are persons assigned male at birth, who identify either as women, not-men, in-between man and woman, or neither man nor woman (the last three may imply what is commonly known as 'third gender'). They may rarely be intersex individuals. They may be considered part of the Indian 'transgender umbrella', but not all transgender persons are hijras. As the explanation shows, hijras are not simply 'male-to-female' transgender people in the Western sense. Contrary to popular belief, all hijras are not castrated or emasculated and 'eunuch' is not an appropriate translation. Hijras have a long tradition and culture of a matrilineal community, membership to which is

a transgender woman thrown out of their home by their biological family.

Equally crucially, the bill fails to address the livelihood concerns of transgender people. Instead of ensuring new opportunities for education and employment, it talks about criminalizing begging—which transgender women prefer to call *chhalla* or *mangti*, a traditional hijra occupation, and one of the few sources of earning they have. The bill also contradicts the internationally accepted standards of care and ethical guidelines issued by the World Professional Association for Transgender Health (based in the US with regional chapters). On the backfoot because of the protests, the government shelved plans to introduce the bill in the December 2017 winter session of Parliament. But the fear is the government, steeped as it is in its barely concealed transphobia, will eventually manage to get it passed with only cosmetic changes.[11]

---

formalized through the ritual of *reet* (christening ceremony). There are several hijra clans or gharanas across South Asia; the term hijra and community norms have many regional variations. Hijra clans consist of gurus and chelas (disciples) who often live in close-knit, rigidly governed, self-created families. It is argued by some that hijra is a cultural and professional identity. Part of Hindu legends and once members of royal courts where they held key positions, hijras fell from grace when British colonists criminalized them. Today, equally feared, reviled and revered by society, they are one of the most disadvantaged communities in South Asia. Apart from the ritualized occupations of *chhalla* or *mangti* (clapping and seeking alms) and *badhai* (blessing newborns and dancing at weddings), which have become intrinsic to their gender identities, many hijras have to depend on exploitative forms of sex work for a living (see, among others, Dhall and Boyce 2015).

11 Even as this volume was being finalized, these fears almost came true when the government rehashed the bill as Transgender Persons (Protection of Rights) Bill, 2018, and got it passed in the Lok Sabha, the lower house of

Aparna should know what she's talking about, given her multiple engagements as a queer activist since the late 1990s, as hijra guru (she joined the hijra community around 10 years ago), as representative of Amitié Trust (a queer support group working in Howrah and Hooghly Districts of West Bengal), and as member of the West Bengal Transgender Development

India's Parliament, on 17 December 2018. By this time the transgender activists gained support from the Opposition parties who promised to try and stall the bill's passage in the Rajya Sabha. But it could not be introduced in the Rajya Sabha within the term of the government at the Centre. After the Bharatiya Janata Party (BJP) coalition won a large majority in the 2019 general elections, it again revised the bill with inadequate attention to civil-society feedback and got it passed without proper debate in the Monsoon Session of the Lok Sabha on 5 August 2019. The bill continued to have major problems. In the definition of 'transgender', it still conflated 'intersex' with 'transgender'. It dropped the 'screening' clause for anyone seeking legal recognition of their gender identity as 'transgender'. But for those assigned female at birth and seeking legal recognition as 'male' or vice versa, it insisted on gender-transition surgery. This was in complete violation of the Supreme Court's *NALSA* verdict. The bill dropped a clause that criminalized begging, but offered little in terms of livelihood. It remained silent on the apex court's directive on reservations for transgender people in education and employment. It also ignored the health concerns of transgender persons, including access to inexpensive and quality gender-transition services. The bill failed to appreciate the concerns of transgender people around family violence and shelter, and its definition of 'family' left out hijra households, which play a crucial role in providing protection to transgender individuals disowned by their natal families. The bill still discriminated against transgender persons in the matter of protection from assault. It proposed a National Council of Transgender Persons, but one heavily skewed towards government representation. Transgender activists and their allies were not looking forward to the bill being tabled in the 2019 Winter Session of the Rajya Sabha. With the ruling coalition gaining ground in the Rajya Sabha, the prospects of a flawed bill becoming law were real and deeply worrisome (see Sampoorna 2019).

Aparna Banerjee speaking at a media conference on the Transgender Persons (Protection of Rights) Bill, 2016 at Kolkata Press Club on 14 December 2017.

Board since its inception in 2015. Apart from tearing through the bill on the aforementioned issues, she focuses on the unfortunate divisions within the transgender communities with regard to the bill. She argues that this split is based not only on the ambitions of some community leaders but, more crucially, on the current political regime's strategy of 'divide and rule'.

Contextualizing the issue in her desire to have a strong voice on anything that relates to transgender communities, she says: 'Hierarchy, autocracy, discrimination are there within the transgender community as well. For that too I have a very strong voice and I'm very rigid about all these things. Take the bill on transgender rights—different levels of activists are

Protests against the Transgender Persons (Protection of Rights) Bill, 2016 during the 16th Kolkata Rainbow Pride Walk on 10 December 2017. *Photograph by Prosenjit Pal.*

involved—some are favouring the bill, some are against. Now, if any activist or community face says that they favour the bill, then that's plain wrong. If lakhs of community members are saying that this bill has been made to destroy the lives of lakhs, then they should take a stand on behalf of all these people and not just for themselves. Maybe somebody fits in with the definition, screening committee, or the rehabilitation part of the bill. But if the person is a leader, they need to understand [issues] as a leader. I will raise my voice against such leaders—they don't even have the sense of leadership.'

When I ask her why some transgender community leaders seem to be taking a pro-government stand in spite of serious and evident shortcomings in the bill, Aparna does not hold back: 'Ever since the bill made an appearance, I've seen that a national cream [sic] of a few leaders has come up, and the hijra term suddenly changed [into] *kinnar*,[12] as if there are no Muslim trans women in India! But the hijra word has an Islamic origin, and you cannot abolish that.[13] This word has come from there, the hijra gharanas, deras have all originated from there. Not all of us are Hindus—because I'm a Muslim, I'm a convert. Being a national leader, you should understand the democracy of the community. There are Dalits too in this, those who do begging. Being a leader, you can't say that begging should be criminalized.

---

12 *Kinnar* is one among several regional variations of the term 'hijra', particularly popular in the Hindi-speaking states of northern India. One explanation of the term would be 'celestial beings that excel at song and dance'. The import of Aparna's comment may be seen reflected in the recent formation of the Kinnar Akhada, a Hindu monastic order of transgender women, which showcased itself at the 2019 Kumbh Mela. While the Kinnar Akhada has been credited with countering the negative stereotypes of transgender persons in the public mind (Lahariya 2019), some transgender activist voices feel it may prove to be divisive along religious lines.

13 'Hijra' as an identity, it has been speculated, derives from 'Hijrah', Prophet Muhammad's emigration in 622 CE from Mecca to Medina to escape persecution. This emigration also represents the start of the Islamic calendar and a new way of life for the Muslims. There is another meaning that emerges from the Persian root *hiz*, meaning 'ineffective' or 'effeminate' (see, among others, Reddy 2005 and Saria 2019). While it has been difficult to establish clearly where the word 'hijra' comes from, it seems more important to recognize the speculation around the word as part of a rising political consciousness among the hijra and other queer communities in South Asia, which have been looking for their own histories.

A Dalit person, man or woman, doesn't get any opportunities, what would a transgender Dalit get in the next 10 years? Can the national leaders define that? Isn't it better to have an inclusive approach that accommodates everyone? Even if everyone doesn't get a hundred rupees each, at least they should all get 12 annas. But these national leaders, when they shout about *kinnar*, are they [not] compartmentalizing the community again? Such divisive politics is killing the whole activism!'[14]

When I first met Aparna, who is among my oldest friends from the queer communities, she was not quite the vocal critic and fiery orator she is today. She was, and still claims to be, 'soft and delicate inside'. The *Anandabazar Patrika* article that helped her discover Counsel Club was the first major exposure for the group in a Bengali daily. It was published in the aftermath of the visibility that queer issues received thanks to the controversy around the film *Fire* in 1998.[15] It brought in a large number of

---

14 At the time of this volume being finalized (August 2019) there seemed to be greater convergence of views among transgender activists about the problems with the latest version of the bill on transgender rights.

15 *Fire*, directed by Deepa Mehta and loosely based on Ismat Chughtai's Urdu short story 'Lihaaf' [Quilt] (published in 1942; see Chughtai 1990: 7–19), was probably the first mainstream Indian film to have depicted same-sex relations explicitly, especially sexual and romantic relations between two women. The Central Board of Film Certification passed it without any cuts. But its release in November 1998 set off furious protests by political and religious groups, which branded it as alien to Indian culture and managed to stop the screening of the film in different cities (Kolkata was possibly one exception where the screening continued unhindered). Several film personalities and human rights activists organized public protests against this not-so-tacit State-supported curtailment of the right to freedom of expression, and petitioned the Supreme Court of India. Eventually police protection was provided for the screenings, but it was not until early 1999 that the screenings resumed without further

The *Anandabazar Patrika* article on 3 April 1999 that featured Counsel Club.

new members to Counsel Club from across the state, and the core group became bigger than it probably ever was. Aparna became part of it and I remember her as quite sociable even then. She was articulate in both English and Bengali, and this seems to have stayed with her. I see this as she takes me through her realizations and turning points in life.

incident. Some feminist and queer support forums were critical of the film for what they felt was a negative depiction of love between two women as resulting from failed marriages. But overall the film created an unprecedented public discourse on homosexuality in India, which had a positive spin-off for queer movements in the country.

The din at New Cathay, an old-time watering hole in central Kolkata quite popular with queer folks, is disconcerting, but Aparna persists: 'When I was growing up, we didn't know anything about gender. When I was in the sixth or seventh class, I was in a relationship with a guy. I used to think I'm a boy but I'm more soft and different from other boys. It wasn't as if there was a girl's sensibility within me, and the term "transgender" wasn't around—it still is very new to me. And I used to be terrified of hijras. I used to think they were born that way. But when I grew up, from school to college, there was a relationship break-up. I faced many questions around my sexuality at home. Being a boy it wasn't considered decent that I should have a sexual relationship with another boy. Eventually I decided to leave my home in Kolkata and went off to Gurgaon [in 2002, to work in a private firm]. I'd often go to Connaught Place to spend time, and there I heard people talking about "transgender", which denoted a gender different from male and female. It was then that the realization dawned on me that though I have the body of a man, my sensibility is not that of a man the way society expects it to be. This is when I began to question and explore myself.

'Three years later [in 2005] I returned to Kolkata as I wanted to be with my friends, but I never went back to my family. I joined an NGO working on sexual rights and HIV interventions. I discovered that many of the friends I had left behind had started cross-dressing, and I felt that this was my own reflection. So I suppose I always had an element of gender dysphoria—I often used to think of the possibility of being a woman, finding love from a man, becoming an air hostess . . .

yeh shareer iss mann se kabhi jur nahin paya uss hadd tak [my body was never quite in alignment with my mind].'

The conversation moves on to the experience around her gender transition, her move towards activism, and how she relates to the issue of pain: 'In 2007 I joined the hijra profession. Many of my friends had already done so. When I started talking to them, I could reaffirm my transgender identity. But I also learnt that if there's any community that's [a] minority in the true sense, then it's this professional community of hijras— which doesn't seek any acknowledgement, always wants to remain in purdah, doesn't want much social attention, development or welfare, and always wants to maintain a mystery around itself. I felt if I wanted to talk about gender in an open forum, then I'd have to be one of them. If I were to take up a job and speak about them, they wouldn't consider me one of them. This motivated me to join the profession.

'Once I was into the hijra profession, I learnt about the frustrations of older community members around gender transition. This would be reflected in comments that since I was educated I'd definitely go for sex-reassignment surgery [rather than the cruder forms of castration and emasculation].[16] But I decided to opt for emasculation and contacted one of the

16 Sex-reassignment (or gender-transition) surgery has slowly been improving in terms of availability, quality, cost and protocol in recent years at least in private hospitals in India. It is a far more scientific process than the cruder forms of castration and emasculation that were practised by hijra communities themselves until recently, or the marginally more 'sophisticated' forms practised by unqualified medical practitioners who thrive because they are less expensive and because of the uncertainty in the hijra and other transgender communities around the legal status of gender-transition procedures.

"doctors" who carry out such operations. The experience was unbearable—if I hadn't gone for it, I wouldn't have known how bad it can be. But later I felt good because this operation gave me intense beautification [sic]. When I see myself through the eyes of others, I feel it has intensely beautified my soul and body.'

Aparna dwells further on her beliefs around why the beautification happened—a mix of thoughts around nirvana (removal of penis and testes is often considered akin to rebirth among hijras), biology of hormones behind feminization, changes in sexual life, and 'gain from pain'.

The last of these is clearly something she relates to closely: 'I'm the same person as I was before, but I received fresh hurt at every new stage in my life and every time this helped me develop a new strategy for survival. After I was able to articulate my gender identity, I started questioning society. It's this society that prevented me from gaining education and moving forward, and that same society dares to come to me for sexual pleasure. This ugly face of society hurt me a lot. If a person is close enough with me to be my sexual partner, even for a one-night stand, then the person should at least have certain responsibility for me. Not in terms of money or kind, but at the end of the day he shouldn't go tell his friends that I'm a *chhakka* [derogatory term for hijras, transgender women in general, or even any man not seen as masculine enough]! Each of these discriminations made me louder, and helped me realize what I'm capable of.'

Going back in time to 1999 again, she cracks a joke about her ignorance when she was under the impression that 'NGO' stood for 'National Gay Organization'. On joining Counsel Club she felt 'for the first time that there are other people like me'. This was her first exposure to the existence of queer support forums, magazines and books. 'In eastern India, Counsel Club was the pioneer, I believe, among all the organizations to start an offline [sic] support group, non-registered, informal support group—for the sexual minorities, I'd say, because gender wasn't talked about much there at that point of time. There was a magazine called *Pravartak*; I also heard about *Trikone Magazine* [one of the earliest queer journals for the South Asian Diaspora started in the US in 1986] and *Bombay Dost*. It was nice to read about ourselves written by people like us. At that time, it was a big deal indeed. When discrimination and violence was much more [prevelant], when keeping such a magazine at home was difficult, we dared to do it! Today there are various social media and channels for people to connect with each other. But then we would wait impatiently for monthly meetings, New Year's Eve parties and Counsel Club's birthday parties. It was so colourful and vibrant! Parties of those times can't happen today, because that thought no longer exists.'

The intense conversation with Aparna leaves me pleasantly exhausted with much to mull over. Queer movements since the 1990s may have impacted her life in many ways, only a few of which could be discussed in our interview. But from a point of time when 'transgender' as a concept was yet to gain clear articulation to now, when a central legislation is being debated on transgender rights in India, Aparna, donning several hats as a champion of transgender communities, seems to be impacting the movements equally or more in return.

Temporal and Spatial Comparisons through Suresh's Story

Social media have a tendency to shrink spaces *and* time. When I met Suresh (name changed) in this coastal city in South India towards the end of November 2017, it did not seem as if the last we'd met was when he was leaving Kolkata in 1998. Perhaps a Skype interview I did with him in 2016 for *Varta* had something to do with it. Touching 70, a part-time teacher of marketing management at a local institute and author of two books on the same subject, Suresh did not appear all that different, never mind the weight, diabetes, painful knees and reduced hearing. The *kada-paak sandesh, panch phoron* masala and *kala jeera* that he asked me to bring from Kolkata did carry with them some nostalgia and added to the glow on his face. We met thrice in three days over some delightful meals—his love for good food and recall of events were intact.

Suresh's shift to another city had left a big hole in the Counsel Club core team and tears in many eyes, including in those of his lover (also a Counsel Club member) whom he met through a personal classified ad in *Pravartak* in 1995. Suresh himself was not very happy about his move, but responsibilities towards his daughter made it unavoidable. He was close to his daughter, although he had married her mother only when, in his early 20s, he could no longer resist family pressure to tie the knot. He nearly came out to his parents and siblings before the marriage, declaring that he was not attracted to girls, but this 'excuse' was summarily dismissed. The marriage ended in divorce after 14 years when Suresh's wife decided to marry another man. Their daughter was around 11 at the time. Nobody knew about his sexual orientation—or perhaps they did not want to know. Nobody still does in his family. His daughter is now settled in Europe.

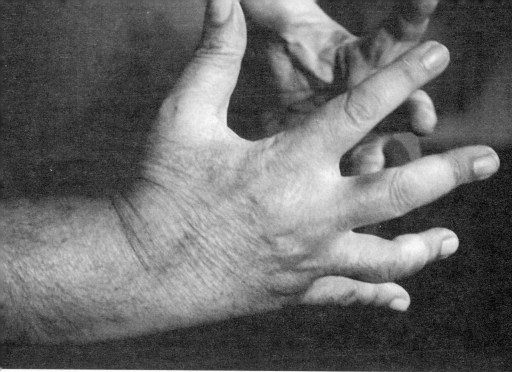

Suresh. *Photograph by Prosenjit Pal.*

Sadly, Suresh's lover could not leave with him because of his own commitments at home, even though he half-expected Suresh to work out an arrangement. Moreover, Suresh was now going to be living at his sister's place and would not have had the independence he enjoyed in Kolkata. Alhough Suresh did keep in touch with his lover and other Counsel Club members through letters and phone calls for a few years, many were deeply disappointed at the fact that the romantic relationship had not lasted. It was not common then, and still is not, that queer people in India get to see a same-sex relationship starting and growing strong right before their eyes.

Introduced to Counsel Club through a founder member in early 1994, Suresh integrated quickly into the group. When Counsel Club started its first Sunday monthly meetings in September 1994, it was Suresh's living room that became the default venue—a safe space and precious resource for the community. Many of the group's collection of books and magazines were also stocked at his place, and the members would read or borrow these during the monthly meetings. Beginning with less than a dozen attendees, the figure grew to around 20 in a year and crossed 30 by 1996. The frequency of the meetings became once every two weeks, but in a year's time Suresh's landlord lost his patience at the 'anti-social activities' afoot under his roof. The meetings moved to another member's place and a hired hall, but Suresh continued to play a key role in the group's activities.

In contrast, Suresh's new hometown had no queer support forums back in 1998. Neither did he have the scope to start something new. He followed key developments in the queer movements through the media. But he was no longer as involved as he once was. Today, though aware of a couple of queer activists in town, he has not felt the urge or energy to network or get involved in any way. On the personal front, barring some casual sexual partners, he has not had a serious relationship in some years. However, it is not as if Suresh's interest in matters sexual has died down. He still talks about it with enthusiasm. Always a votary for 'good sex' and same-sex relationships (if not marriages), he believes that one should be relaxed about sexual fidelity—a 'little playing around' only 'adds spice' to life as he was once quoted in an article in *Pravartak* on ageing among gay men (Sanjay 1997–98).

A student of chemistry honours, he remembered college being a dull affair in terms of sexual experiences. There were deep friendships but nothing sexual—and all was hush-hush. Though he knew about one of Kolkata's most popular cruising sites, a public park not far from home, Suresh never dared to go there till much later (after joining Counsel Club). School days were better, when playing 'dark room' at a friend's place allowed for fooling around. After graduation, a marketing job in an industrial-gases company took him to Mumbai and work trips across India before bringing him to Kolkata in the 1970s. These travels were replete with sexual encounters with 'room boys' in hotels. There was also an instance of unrequited love with a roommate in Mumbai. These experiences stopped when Suresh got married in Kolkata. After his divorce, he resumed hooking up with other men—first in Guwahati (where he was then posted) and later when he returned to Kolkata.

By the time he joined Counsel Club, he was not even looking for much in terms of partners, but then he met the man with whom he spent some of the best years of his life. His partner was from a town in North 24 Parganas District of West Bengal, but he moved in with Suresh in his South Kolkata home. 'I've never had such an experience ever again,' rued Suresh. After leaving Kolkata in 1998, Suresh did make a few trips to back to the city (to visit his brother) and Guwahati, but did not meet his old lover or the majority of other Counsel Club friends, including me. I was curious to know why but detected a note of sadness or reluctance on his part, so I did not press further.

Suresh was more animated talking about why intergenerational relationships among gay men were on the rise: 'more openness among gay men now, but also socioeconomic factors'; as well as about the changes in popular sexual parlance: '"active–passive" has given way to "top–bottom" and there was no "versatile" in our times'. He felt there was greater freedom of expression among queer people and personal liberty now than in his younger days, and had an interesting take on the matter: 'There are more options like social media and dating apps now for finding sexual or romantic

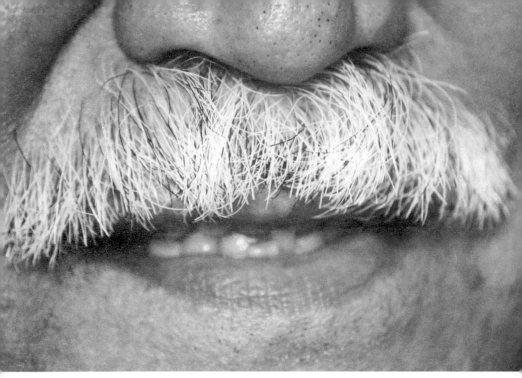

Suresh. *Photograph by Prosenjit Pal.*

partners. More openness among gay people means there's more demand for safe spaces for sex, and the hospitality industry is tapping into this demand in different ways!' Of course, who enjoys the access to these 'safe spaces' depends on which city or which part of the city one is in, and certainly on one's gender. But our discussion did not venture into this area.

Earlier in the conversation he talked about Kolkata Police's *khochors* in the 1990s—a term coined by the public, 'police's kept' in Suresh's words. They would do the 'dirty work' that the police could officially not do, such as harassing and extorting money from couples (same-sex or otherwise) in public parks in the name of law and order. He recollected an instance when Counsel Club members trying to have an evening meeting in the park opposite Victoria Memorial, popularly known as Maidan, were chased away by a group of such agents. This was how laws such as Section 377 of the Indian Penal Code helped persecute queer people, he said, adding that there was 'a long way to go' for queer movements, but they should also 'spare a thought for older queer people'. After goodbyes at the railway station, as Suresh walked away, I could have sat on a bench and ruminated for hours—about all the work that had been done as part of Counsel Club, the successes and failures over the years, and the debates and disputes that were an inevitable part of these processes.

Often the disagreements we as members of Counsel Club had with one another arose from our expectations about how the group should function *and* how each member should function in the interest of the group. Sometimes even our personal sexual ethics and lives came under scrutiny. There were often no easy resolutions, perhaps because we were still not fully familiar with concepts like organizational policies that could have acted as a guide. It was only towards the last couple of years of Counsel Club that we tried to frame such policies. By that time Suresh had left Kolkata. But while he was around, as a senior figure even in those years, he had an image of neutrality and his inputs during meetings provided a sense of assurance.

Part of me wanted to continue conversing with Suresh and bring up issues that were never resolved so many years ago. It was as if two decades having passed by meant nothing and I could have readily flown back on a river of memories and half-memories. But there was a train to catch moving in the opposite direction, and a story to write.

I first travelled to this town in the Nuapada District of western Odisha in October 2000. I was luckier than long-legs Ranjan, a colleague at Counsel Club and sister NGO Integration Society (formed in early 1999),[17] in negotiating the 14-hour cramped bus journey from Bhubaneswar to ABC Nagar. (I am not allowed to reveal any obvious identity marker by interviewee Anubhav, also an alias.) The trip was also the beginning of my enduring love affair with work and travels in one of the most scenic states in India.

Seventeen years later, the journey to ABC Nagar, at the end of September 2017, was longer in terms of distance—by overnight train from Bhubaneswar to Bhawanipatna, and then another couple of hours by bus to my final destination. But it was more comfortable and, if one does not consider the overnight halt at Bhawanipatna, actually faster as the travel time was just about the same as in 2000. Also, on the first occasion, the journey from Bhubaneswar was preceded by six hours of train travel from Kolkata and a couple of days' stay in Bhubaneswar. This time I flew early morning from Kolkata to Bhubaneswar and was on the train to Bhawanipatna the same evening.

Ranjan and I parted ways as colleagues around 2002 when I left both Counsel Club and Integration Society. So this time I was on my own. But Anubhav was there to meet me in Bhawanipatna and take me to ABC Nagar, just as he had met

---

17 While Counsel Club functioned as a non-registered, community-funded safe meeting and socializing space for queer people, Integration Society was a registered body that focused on provision of health, legal aid and related services to queer communities. Integration Society was formed in 1999 and functioned till at least 2005.

us in Bhubaneswar then and accompanied us on the bus journey to his home and a nearby guest house.

Both the journeys were photographic delights, but the
need for confidentiality means I am unable to present a visual
comparison in the changes I could make out in ABC Nagar.
Generally speaking, though, one obvious change was, of course,
that the town had expanded and become much more built-up
and crowded. Almost as a corollary, it had lost greenery and was
dustier, dirtier and more strewn with plastic bags; the poor quality of the roads lent it a more broken-down look. The start and
end points of the trip from Bhawanipatna to ABC Nagar, the
respective bus stands, were exceptionally dirty, with no visible
sign of the central government's much-touted Swachh Bharat
[Clean India] movement anywhere.

I missed the green overhang that was everywhere we went
in 2000—it lent a near spookiness to the guesthouse where I
had stayed, not least because the road in front used to be quite
deserted. This time around I did not get to visit the guesthouse;
neither could I experience the thrill of 'mini' rock climbing on
the outskirts of the town and the sight of young men using bun-
dles of leafy weeds to slide down 30 feet on the smooth surface
of a rock formation. A bike trip, courtesy Anubhav's neighbour,
to a nearby multipurpose river-valley project and a dhaba meal
en route did compensate somewhat. I also experienced a bit of
the Durga Puja fervour far away from Bengal, sweetened further with freshly made hot jalebis on the roadside. But on the
whole the initial part of the second visit to ABC Nagar was disconcerting in many ways.

My conversation with Anubhav began in Bhawanipatna
itself, but on reaching his home it proved tough to get him to

talk at any length. Work-related distractions (he is a senior official in a cooperative rural bank in ABC Nagar) and incessant messages and Facebook pings on his mobile phone would come in the way. Most of his family was visiting Bhawanipatna—where I'd met them with Anubhav over a meal the previous day—and managing the household, trying to fix a burnt-out water-pump connection, and hospitality for me created further worries. Eventually, when we did get some time to talk, it was only after he had returned from work, given me a short evening tour of the town, bought some household stuff, and after I had convinced him (and his wife over phone) to let me cook egg bhurji to go with his chapattis for dinner.

Once the conversation started, he was reluctant to have the interview digitally recorded. Moreover, with the stop-start conversation stretched over nearly three days, it meant that the recorder could not be kept on all through. Our reminiscing took us back to 1996, when a 30-year-old and married Anubhav contacted Counsel Club through an interestingly circuitous route. I mentioned our initial correspondence, which began with him writing in to publish a personal classified ad in *Pravartak*. It gave the impression that though he knew other queer individuals even then, he seemed quite isolated given that he was in a remote location. But Anubhav debunked my argument and said that he was 'rather excited' when he first wrote in.

His interest in films and making pen pals brought him in touch with a Hindi magazine called *Chitrakatha*, where he was shocked to find some advertisers openly mention their '*samlingta ke prati aakarshan*' [attraction towards the same sex]. Thus far he had always thought of it—including his own intimate experiences and attractions—as something confined to

jokes and jibes between boys in school and college. These
instances of frank self-expression developed a new '*ruchi*' [inter-
est] in him, which led to new friendships and subscription to
another Hindi magazine called *Madhur Katha*. This in turn
made him aware of *Bombay Dost*, from where he came to know
a young gay man in Cuttack who was already in touch with
Counsel Club and introduced him to the support group.

Among memories of Counsel Club, Anubhav spoke fondly
of some group members from Kolkata, and the three Network
East events organized by Counsel Club in 1997, 1999 and 2002
(the last two together with Integration Society). These were eastern India regional meets inspired by one of India's first confer-
ences for gay and other men who have sex with men (MSM)[18]

---

18 As the *Wikipedia* says, MSM stands for 'men who have sex with men' (some
people prefer 'males who have sex with males' to account for the fact that male-
to-male sex is not restricted to adults). This term was coined in the public-
health context in the early 1990s to stand for male persons who engage
in sexual activity with members of the same sex, regardless of how they identify themselves. This could be gay, bisexual, homosexual, even straight or heterosexual, or none of these sexual-identity terms, or even no particular term
at all. In a narrow biological sense, even transgender women who have sex
with men, given their presumably male anatomy by birth, used to be included
among MSM by public-health professionals. But since the 2000s, transgender
women have strongly opposed such conflation on justifiable grounds because
it leads to invisibilization of their sociocultural identities as well as specific
health concerns at both policy and programmatic levels. In the context of
India's National AIDS Control Programme, it was only from its fourth phase
since 2011–12 that transgender women were considered separately from MSM
for targeted HIV interventions. Over the years, the public-health rationale of
looking at MSM in an identity-neutral sense has worn thin as even gay and
bisexual men have argued that the term invisibilizes their sociocultural con-
texts and well-being concerns.

organized in Mumbai in 1994 by Humsafar Trust and Naz Project, London. Mumbai-based Humsafar Trust was another early starter as an Indian queer support group led by well-known activist and journalist Ashok Row Kavi, while Naz Project was an international NGO focused on sexual-health concerns of queer communities in the Global South led by the late Shivananda Khan, who had roots in Bengal and was then settled in the UK.

The Network East events brought together queer individuals from throughout the region (and even across the border from Nepal) for networking, experience sharing, sexual-health and human rights workshops, as well as entertainment. Anubhav was one of the few who attended all three editions of Network East, and the experience of the first two led him to mobilize a small group of men in and around ABC Nagar to form a local queer support group sometime in early 2000. It was a training session with them that brought Ranjan and me to ABC Nagar later that same year. With memories of Mamata and Monalisa still quite fresh, we were hopeful that possibly the first attempt at forming a queer support forum in Odisha would go a long way. Not that we expected Anubhav to be able to mobilize queer women also at the outset (his connections were limited to men), but things could have worked out over time. This, however, was not to be.

Anubhav's venture made a promising start, bringing more than half a dozen men in their 20s and 30s together at monthly meetings and getting registered with the district administration as an AIDS awareness group. Over the next couple of years, the group participated in some of the cultural, fundraising and training events organized by Counsel Club and Integration

Society in Kolkata (including the last Network East conference in January 2002). Anubhav would be a constant figure and brought along one or two of the other group members each time. My correspondence with Anubhav during these years shows considerable exchange of information and ideas on how to manage and take forward the emerging support group. They also attempted HIV/AIDS awareness activities and networking with other NGOs locally in Nuapada District.

However, the group had inherent contradictions that soon started showing up. For one, Anubhav found himself somewhat cornered in the group. The majority of the other members were not keen on talking much about gender, sexuality and sexual-health issues. Many could not relate to the need to be together in relation to such issues, especially when they had never faced any problems around their sexual preferences. A few members may also have had expectations of earning money through the group, which was not surprising since NGOs were (and still are) often seen as rich in resources. The Indian national HIV/AIDS response was still in its early stages, but the fact that it was well funded was fast becoming common knowledge.

In Anubhav's words, 'Our group was never quite a gay support group; it was more of an AIDS awareness group. The members didn't take their own same-sex sexual interests, behaviours or relationships quite seriously.' What could have been the reason for this? Anubhav was not very forthcoming, but one can surmise a number of factors at play. Socio-legal stigma for one—it discourages people from being open about their sexual orientation and gender identity. For married queer individuals, the going can be tougher, and many of Anubhav's fellow members were either married or going to be married in the future; he himself was married and a father of two at that time.

Another reason could have been male privilege at play, at least for some of the group's members. Irrespective of their marital status they could, if they wanted, easily find male or transgender sexual partners or love interests in ABC Nagar, without quite having to worry about answering any uncomfortable questions. Add to that a homosocial but heteronormative cultural milieu, and (homo- or bi-) sexual orientation would have been a rather alien concept as a marker for community mobilization in the context of ABC Nagar.

In my understanding, even Anubhav himself was never fully convinced about the support group's focus. Perhaps this was related to his ambivalence towards his own sexuality. Whether back in the days of Counsel Club and Integration Society or now, he never spoke about his sexuality to anyone in his family, including his wife. This could well be out of fear of social ostracization, though one cannot discount his desire for fluidity around his sexuality irrespective of any social pressure.

Then again, his narrative of intimacies and relationships in his growing-up and later years included both women and men, but the emphasis was clearly on men. One of the most intense relationships he had was with an older male cousin, which seemed to have included elements of romantic role play. Yet he said he could not imagine a long-term relationship with a man.

He emphasized that he did not marry under any compulsion. Rather, it was his love for children that motivated him to overcome all doubts and get married. At the same time, he talked at length about his social-media networking with younger men till date. After a while Anubhav's narration of his friendships and relationships seemed to veer off track again and again, getting lost in random details, and I felt it best to discuss other issues.

Coming back to the support group, it ultimately wound up sometime in 2003 or 2004. Sadly, it did not succeed even in its official objective of generating HIV/AIDS awareness, which was neither misplaced nor disconnected from issues of gender and sexuality. After all, queer communities, especially MSM and transgender women, are among the worst affected by the HIV epidemic and it is the stigma, discrimination and violence around their non-normative genders and sexualities that renders them particularly vulnerable to HIV exposure and impact of the epidemic.

Moreover, adopting HIV/AIDS awareness as a key objective used to be a common strategy for queer support groups in the 1990s and 2000s. It helped avoid socio-legal stigma, obtain government registration and raise much-needed resources for sexual health and human rights interventions. And while HIV and AIDS carried their own social stigma, government engagement with the issue and the national HIV programme's 'targeted interventions' for (already) criminalized groups such as sex workers, injecting drug users, MSM and transgender women, albeit problematic at several levels, provided HIV/AIDS awareness work some 'validity'.

Veena Lakhumalani on Tackling the West Bengal Government's Denial That Homosexuality Existed in the State

While narrating how the West Bengal Sexual Health Project (WBSHP) came to be in the mid 1990s, Veena spoke about her own initial scepticism towards the reality of an HIV epidemic in the state. This was in 1991–92 when she was involved in a campaign around issues of drug use. However, as the epidemic made its presence felt, it was an eye-opener and she educated herself about the vulnerability of different communities to HIV.

The next challenge was around understanding and being able to explain the concept of 'sexual health'—to not just the vulnerable communities but also to government officials, health practitioners and social workers. This was crucial because even as early as then it was clear that tackling HIV was not just a medical issue. Seen in the light of sexual health, tackling HIV also demanded paying attention to mental health and social well-being. This in turn meant eliminating stigma and discrimination against the people most vulnerable to HIV and, even before that, acknowledging that they existed amid us. Veena spoke about her run-in with a government official hell-bent on denying the existence of gay men in Bengal:

'At the early stages of this work that we were doing before we started the WBSHP, I remember a meeting at the Calcutta School of Tropical Medicine. I was already involved with Counsel Club, and there at the meeting there was complete denial by an official from the Government of West Bengal that there were gay people in India. I stood up and said excuse me, I have something to say. And I said, What do you mean there are no gay people in India? There are plenty of them in India. He said, Oh but we don't have them in West

Bengal. I said, I'm talking about Calcutta, and he said, Then they're not Bengalis!

'One of the things I deliberately did when we started the project and began interacting with the government was to encourage Debanuj, who had participated in all our trainings—he hadn't come out publicly at that stage, so every conference meeting I would make him sit near the guy from the government, the deputy secretary–health. I said you tell him when you are ready that you are from the gay community. So it came as a shock to the official, and he said, Why didn't you tell me? So I asked him has it changed your opinion about him—has he got horns or has he got a tail? He's still a human being.'

Subsequent to this and similar other incidents, Veena felt there was an attitudinal change in some government officials, at least in private. The WBSHP began supporting research projects among MSM, but it was not till 1999 that MSM were included in the National AIDS Control Programme, and it was only in 2004 that the West Bengal government funded the first large-scale HIV intervention among MSM in the state, many years after similar support was extended to other vulnerable communities.

ABC Nagar was located on a major highway for truckers, and some of them were likely to have been clients of sex workers living along or near the highway. With unprotected sex between truckers and sex workers known to be common, ABC Nagar could not have been a stranger to HIV. I remember, during our 2000 trip, Anubhav and others escorting Ranjan and me to an open air, all-night music-and-dance show near a major truck depot. There were young women gyrating to a raunchy number on a high stage for an almost all-male audience. The hour or so we spent there also made male-to-male sexual cruising a distinct possibility at or near the site. Later, my work over more than a decade (2002–14) with an NGO called SAATHII (Solidarity and Action Against The HIV Infection in India), which focused on strengthening civil society and government HIV responses, corroborated our perception of ABC Nagar and Nuapada District's vulnerability to the HIV epidemic.

In 2017, when I reminded Anubhav about these experiences and the potential the support group had, he explained: 'So much work was done to obtain the registration, but people lost interest because the government schemes we applied for didn't yield any immediate results. Besides, I had my job and so did the others, most of them young and restless. We lost steam.'

I also detected a note of grouse Anubhav seemed to have, possibly because the support group had greater expectations of funding support from Counsel Club and Integration Society in Kolkata. The grouse also seemed to be a personal one because I had failed to meet Anubhav when he visited Kolkata with his family en route a trip to North Bengal. I apologized for both, and explained that Integration Society had a mandate to facilitate fundraising through grants rather than itself provide funds. Perhaps this aspect was not clearly communicated those many years ago. But by now it was too late. As Anubhav said, all but two members of the support group had left ABC Nagar and, given the short duration of my trip, I missed meeting the only other one around.

* * *

On the morning of the day I was supposed to return to Kolkata from ABC Nagar via Bhawanipatna and Bhubaneswar, I wondered what had come off the trip. The conversation with Anubhav had been engrossing but difficult to conduct. He had sounded far more welcoming over phone and email when I had explained the purpose of my trip and sought his consent for the interview.

I respected his insistence on camouflaging the name of his town, which was also his birthplace, but it also seemed to rob the charm of writing about travelling back in time. My memories of a happy and large household—partly fossilized in photographs in the Counsel Club archives—were now subdued by the reality of time, people growing old and infirm, the young growing up and going away, friends no longer around.

In 2000, I had met Anubhav, his wife, their daughter in early childhood and infant son, Anubhav's widowed mother, his sister and her husband and their children. In one of the old pictures, I had Anubhav's son in my arms—there had been much laughter when I mixed up the genders of the boy and his sister. Anubhav's house was then being built and his sister's home in the adjacent plot had been the site of many a happy meal. The training session with the support group took place in one of the rooms in Anubhav's incomplete house. Now, in 2017, the sprawling two-storey house and surrounding courtyard and garden seemed sadly empty. Part of the ground floor and the upper floors had a few tenants. Anubhav's mother was too frail to move around on her own (she seemed to vaguely recognize me and smiled); his sister was still his neighbour, and we did have one quite heavy 'throwback' meal at her place.

But his daughter and elder son were both pursuing higher studies in faraway cities; a second son born some years after my first trip still lived with Anubhav and his wife.

As I mulled over these thoughts with the morning tea, Anubhav sprang a surprise! Amid his ramblings that I was now familiar with, he revealed that he had often spoken to his daughter, the eldest of his three children, about his engagement with HIV/AIDS issues—though not about the queer angle to his engagement. She had seen him involved in the local support group's activities as well as make trips to Kolkata years ago. She was now pursuing a course in social sciences and, in fact, still remembered Ranjan and me and wanted to say hello over the phone. Over the next hour and more what followed was one of the most endearing phone calls I have ever had, and it quite changed the complexion of the trip.

Anubhav's daughter credited him for having spoken to her about transgender and other queer people right from her childhood, often in the context of the HIV/AIDS awareness work of the NGO he had once set up. It was her father who taught her to look at transgender women as just like any other human being. She shared that she had no hesitation in striking up a conversation with hijras seeking alms on trains, much to the consternation and embarrassment of her brother, Anubhav's second child.

She had also run afoul of her college mates when she empathized with transgender people in a writing assignment, and said she could not comprehend their homophobia and transphobia. Time flew as I answered questions on gender and sexuality diversity and the nature of my work. She wanted reading references, and thanked me for having chosen to come to ABC Nagar to research this volume. On my part, I uttered a silent thank you to Anubhav. What he had achieved with his daughter was not just a personal and parental success, but also something that queer movements anywhere yearn for—inclusive and accepting attitudes in people! I wished I could have met her along with her brothers in Bhawanipatna. I also wondered why Anubhav had let his sons grow up with the usual insecurities associated with so many boys and men.

A boxful of heavenly *pedas* from a popular confectioner in town was not my only takeaway as Anubhav and I began a hired-car journey back to Bhawanipatna. I had developed a strange and grudging new respect for my fellow traveller. He was not without his quirks and patriarchal biases like all of us. (Example: he did not want his children, when they were young, to seé sex workers living in the neighbourhood.) His stand on his sexuality and marriage might not be appreciated by many, and I never got around to hearing his wife's perspective on different issues discussed with Anubhav. But what if things were seen in a perspective besides or parallel to these issues?

Anubhav never had the desire to move out of his birthplace, happy to have his office never far from home. He was content that he had done all that was expected of him—got married, educated his children, built a house for his family, taken care of the elderly at home, organized family holiday tours. But then he had done some more! His support group venture, however flawed and short-lived, with minimal access to resources in a small town nearly two decades ago is hardly talked about in queer discourse today. Yet it did contribute to lessons learnt and to the tapestry of eastern India's queer movements. And should not the life education he provided his daughter be counted as something remarkable?

Trajectory of the Earliest Queer Support Groups in Odisha

My stopover at Bhawanipatna, the headquarters of Kalahandi District, en route to ABC Nagar was significant in many ways. The day I arrived in town from Bhubaneswar, all traffic to the city centre was diverted to accommodate large Chatar Jatra processions. These are brought out annually in worship of goddess Maa Manikeswari and overlap with Durga Puja festivities in Kalahandi District. I had been forewarned and so was prepared to walk about a kilometre to the hotel from where the auto-rickshaw dropped me. Nonetheless, negotiating the crowds was a challenge, more so with animal sacrifice being carried out along the procession routes—mostly hens, in some cases goats, and often coconuts as a symbolic substitute for the first two.

What also caught my attention was the fervour among the processionists, a large section of which seemed to include young men in their 20s and 30s. Some of the people I inter-acted with in Odisha during the trip, including Anubhav, were critical of the open display of animal sacrifice and the image of Kalahandi that it seemed to convey. This tied in with the past assertions of ex-colleagues from SAATHII in Odisha who argued that the portrayal of Kalahandi as 'backward' in the media was outdated. But based on two brief visits, both limited to Bhawanipatna town (the first in 2012 as part of my work in SAATHII), all I could make out was the usual jostling of 'tradi-tion' and 'modernity' that marks all urban India.

From my vantage point, the town and the district were more significant for having been the site of Bhawanis, a support group for MSM and transgender women that begun around 2005. Quite possibly this initiative was the first of its kind to have started and sustained in Odisha after Anubhav's venture ran aground. I got an opportunity to meet and interact with key members of the group only by 2008–09, and almost immediately took a liking for their tenacity and warmth. Among them was Dambarudhar Sunani, who in her own quiet way worked persistently for Bhawanis till her unexpected death in May 2014 (Dhall 2014). Among the earliest transgender activist voices in Odisha, her end came about because of depression around a chronic disease—she would often discontinue her medication for long periods of time. The group lost another founder member within a year or so for similar reasons. Their passing away held an important lesson for the queer movements to focus more on mental-health interventions.

During this visit, I met the last surviving founder member of Bhawanis, though not specifically for the purpose of this book. The support group was carrying on with its monthly meetings and other activities, but perhaps not as vigorously. It had recently severed ties with a partner NGO that the group felt had let them down. The promises made by the NGO in helping Bhawanis with organizational development had not materialized. These promises were part of a partnership under Project Pehchan, which aimed to build the capacity of 200 community-based organizations (CBOs) across India to provide sexual-health services to MSM and transgender women communities. The five-year project, funded by the Global Fund to Fight AIDS, Tuberculosis and Malaria and designed in line with the National

AIDS Control Programme, had stringent financial-management requirements that made it necessary for CBOs like Bhawanis to depend on better-established NGOs for fiscal partnerships. This often turned out to be a grossly unequal relationship loaded against the very CBO that was supposed to be helped, and which more often than not would be led by individuals with limited access to education and other resources. With the closure of Project Pehchan in 2016, the partner NGO of Bhawanis seemed to have lost interest, and the group was now on its own. Yet, it had not given up and could still fall back on the experience of more than a decade of functioning—not to discount the staying power of its members, all survivors of stigma, discrimination and violence in different social spheres, including their livelihoods, sex work and traditional hijra occupations being the commonest.

The story of Bhawanis was repeated in the Bhadrak District of Odisha—with Santi Seva, another support group exclusively for hijras and other transgender women which started in 2006. As part of my work in SAATHII, Santi Seva was among the groups I was most invested in. I had been involved in its formation and functioning over eight years from the days of the group's foundation meetings. Working with the six founding members of the group (all in their 40s or 50s in 2006), including Sheikh Jalaluddin or Jaina Nani, guru to the hijra community in Bhadrak Town, was a humbling experience.

Some of my transgender colleagues in SAATHII shared an affinity with the community at the level of a sisterhood, which was an eye-opener for others in the organization. We worked with Jaina and others to understand the community's priorities and challenges, and help them establish Santi Seva as their

beacon of hope. In the process, I learnt how the community
members negotiated family ties, relations with neighbours,
extremely restricted incomes and limited livelihood options,
insecurity around food and shelter, health problems (including
HIV, mental illnesses and substance use), and intra-community
rivalries (particularly when there was 'encroachment' into one
another's areas of operations for *badhai* and *chhalla*). I also
learnt about their sex lives and romantic flings with the men of
the town across age groups. I got glimpses of their festivities,
as well as soul-satisfying kebab treats from Jaina every time I
visited Bhadrak.

We attempted to tie up Santi Seva's activities closely to the
community's day-to-day priorities. This meant focusing on
learning reading, writing and arithmetic, facilitating access to
social-security services, and organizing health camps, which,
being open to all, were also a means for the community to build
goodwill with the larger populace of Bhadrak. For several years,
Santi Seva ran a self-help group that enabled its members
access to easy credit for their small trades—tea and grocery
shops, poultry farming, flower-decoration services, bicycle-
repair shops and the like—or to meet emergency health and
household-repair expenses.

There were failures and setbacks aplenty. Dropouts from
different group activities were common; non-repayment of
loans taken from the self-help group a constant headache.
Health-seeking behaviours improved, but the group still lost
key members to HIV and alcoholism. Santi Seva's membership
expanded well beyond Bhadrak Town into the remote corners
of the district. The group even inspired the formation of a sister
group called Santi Sena in neighbouring Jajpur District, where

the community once was at loggerheads with hijras in Bhadrak. But a larger scale of operations also meant challenges in managing conflicting priorities. Tensions would often flare up as the younger community members were critical of the older lot's approach, including Jaina's leadership. When Santi Seva became registered as a charitable trust, its organizational management and statutory compliances had their share of demands.

None of these challenges would have been insurmountable, but for a let-down by one of Santi Seva's key partner NGOs in Bhadrak—an agency with almost three decades of experience. To its credit, this NGO acted as a 'parent' to Santi Seva right from the start in 2006—it was through this NGO's outreach activities under a government-funded HIV intervention that Santi Seva's founder members were accessed and motivated to sit together. For the first five years or so, the NGO provided office, training and drop-in centre space for the group. It also acted as the group's local fiscal partner, given that Santi Seva was not in a position to receive funds into its own bank account from SAATHII or any donor agency. But fortunately for Santi Seva, it was not entirely dependent on this one NGO. It had always had strong parallel links with SAATHII, especially through a project that was supported by a donor happy to see qualitative and incremental progress rather than the bluster of quantitative data.

This provided time and space for Santi Seva's leadership to grow with a certain degree of independence that seemed to not go down well with the partner NGO. Matters almost came to a head when Santi Seva and SAATHII questioned suspected anomalies in the partner NGO's financial management. It was

heartening to see Santi Seva develop a sense of ownership for
funds that were rightfully theirs! Ultimately, Santi Seva chose
to avoid an outright confrontation with the NGO. But this was
more as a matter of gratitude for the NGO's founder, who had
long been a benefactor to Jaina and her fellow community
members. We in SAATHII respected Santi Seva's choice as we
did not have an organizational base in Bhadrak. However, this
incident also brought to the fore barely concealed transphobia
and class bias in the NGO. When in about a year (2010–11)
Project Pehchan came calling, Santi Seva decided to make a
break from the past and moved into its own office with support
from SAATHII. Eventually, when all its income-tax registrations
fell into place, the group no longer needed to depend on the
NGO to receive funds from at least any Indian donor or partner
agency.

It probably was extreme naivety to have not expected nega-
tivity from the NGO. Santi Seva's own leadership and staff
members included individuals under significant influence of
the NGO. Many of the staff had earlier been employed by the
NGO to work on Santi Seva's projects. They seemed to play up
the tension between a younger hijra leader from the outskirts
of Bhadrak and Jaina. Conflicts between Santi Seva's leadership
and staff became frequent, which began telling on different project outputs. A senior official affiliated to the NGO even tried
intimidating SAATHII's staff members from Bhubaneswar and
Kolkata. The final blow came when Santi Seva's office was emp-
tied of all its assets by some of the staff members and Jaina's
detractors within the transgender community. Police com-
plaints yielded some recoveries, but the upshot was near closure
of all projects and activities at Santi Seva by 2015.

By the time the worst happened, I had left SAATHII. When an ex-colleague, someone who also saw Santi Seva grow through the years, narrated these developments to me, it seemed hard to believe. He was in tears as he remembered the earliest years (2003–04) when we would travel together to Bhadrak to begin SAATHII's operations in Odisha—ironically in collaboration with the very NGO that had now become estranged. But for me the reality truly sunk in when I made a trip in December 2017 to Bhadrak and saw and heard first-hand what had transpired. Santi Seva's office was in shambles. Their bank savings allowed them to rent only one room in a building where once they had rented two floors, albeit small ones by big-city standards. Only one staff member remained to manage the accounts and file annual returns of income.

What had not changed were Jaina and her faithful lot of friends. I and others with me were treated with the same warmth and hospitality. What had also not changed were the living conditions of many of Santi Seva's members. It seemed like a painful story of what could have been. This was a reality check that brought home the futility of some of the approaches of our 'development' work and social movements. How far are we willing to let go of our powers and privileges and get our hands dirty? What price are we willing to pay for demanding accountability? How far are we willing to fight back when the power structures try to suppress us? Do the queer movements in eastern India introspect on the power structures and lack of accountability within their own circles?

I know I will be going back to Bhadrak. For the sake of the gentle soul that is Jaina—not only a hijra guru but also the loving eldest 'son' in her family who passed on all her share of the family property to her younger siblings, and now just has one room to herself in the entire house. This one room opens out onto the street, allowing Jaina her independence and ready access to the outer world. I look forward to meeting her here again over tea and perhaps kebabs as well. Perhaps we will revive Santi Seva's monthly meetings. Perhaps there will be Jaina and just her immediate hijra family at the meeting, only a few people. That was how it all began more than a decade ago; or, for that matter, in the early 1990s.

* * *

This story has to go back to Meenakshi and Jyoti one more time.

The essence of being queer has to be more than to unsettle the compulsory heterosexuality thrust on us day in and day out. If there is something called heteronormativity, then there is also homonormativity, which can be just as restrictive in telling queer people how they should be queer. So it seems queer is something that must also question its own queerness. Meenakshi's life seems to reflect this reality.

Meenakshi and Jyoti's story did not have a happy Bollywood ending. For Meenakshi, her relationship with Jyoti and the decision to move to Delhi was the 'first choice [she] ever made in life'. Prior to this everything was pre-decided for her by somebody else. She felt she would have given in to her father's manipulations and exhortations 'in Manu's name' to get her married. But being with Jyoti gave her the courage to go in for a 'direct confrontation with patriarchy'.

Yet, within a couple of years, what Meenakshi had with Jyoti seemed to have been lost. So far their energies had been spent on ensuring that they could be together. As they began to live out and explore their relationship, their 'goals' began to differ. As Meenakshi progressed professionally, she wanted to have a life beyond their little world. 'I wanted to grow with the relationship, but the other person wasn't willing to do the same. Jyoti became very possessive.'

Our conversation slowed down as Meenakshi grappled with memories and emotions: 'It was gradual and a tough decision to take. We'd been through so much—we'd left our families, home town and culture for this one relationship. How could we just separate? What would we tell the world? How would we face our friends? I was also under this pressure—am I going to end up proving that such relationships don't last? Then over a period of time, she became so vulnerable and I would feel that there was no one else to take care of her. Or I used to feel that it's my responsibility, and I was made to feel that I was responsible. And, of course, because we entered the relationship with this commitment that we'd be together forever and never break up.'

Sadly, it was Meenakshi's work—frequent out-of-town trips for training sessions—that acted as a trigger. Jyoti would complain that Meenakshi was never there when she needed her. In Meenakshi's mind, it was ironically once again all about independence: 'As long as I was dependent on her, things were all right. But when I was able to make my own way forward, there were problems.' Yet another manifestation of patriarchy? I asked. But Meenakshi said, 'It wasn't even clearly that. It wasn't as if she had a masculine persona. It was more subtle, and I'd feel guilty. For instance, I couldn't come home and say, "Hey, I had a great day." I couldn't have a separate friend circle, or say yes to a get-together if she didn't feel like going.'

Meenakshi felt that today, even as she spoke to me, she was able to look at things more dispassionately. But back then, it was all about trying to save the relationship at any cost— through love, affection, adjustments, compromises. It was after all about a shared personal history, something they were both proud of. And it was endearing to see that Meenakshi would still often refer to Jyoti with the respectful *unhone* or *unko* pronoun in Hindi rather than use her name.

Eventually, things got worse. For one, Meenakshi became more assertive and began to look at and question their relationship through the lens of equity. At the same time, Jyoti left her full-time job around 2000 and started freelance work, which would at best be erratic in terms of earnings. She continued to freelance for the next 10 years till their break-up. Meenakshi felt her attitude of not wanting to make adjustments in her work was quite unreasonable.

Along the way, anger took over Meenakshi. She could not express her helplessness at trying to run the household almost singlehandedly. This was also the time when they had bought their own flat, with generous interest-free loans from friends and colleagues. The additional pressure of expenses involved in further study courses began telling on her nerves. At this stage they sought counselling support, which they could not agree on earlier. A couple of close friends also tried to help. Suggestions were made for the two to live apart for a while. Yet, nothing worked and Meenakshi was still continuously reminded that they were supposed to stick it out together. Finally, around 2004,

Meenakshi had to admit to herself: 'This is not the person I had loved.' But it took another six years for her to 'untie' all bonds, emotional as well as mundane financial matters, and walk out of the relationship completely.

Something else happened around the same time. A sense of wonderment crept into Meenakshi's voice as she said: 'I don't know what to make out of the way things happened with me. In 2004, eight years since I left home, I reconciled with my family, especially my mother. I contacted them because I was determined that now that I'm established, I don't feel ashamed about myself, I'm proud of my work and relationship, I have my house, so I'm not anybody's liability. So I felt I should approach and tell them that this kind of a life also exists and that they should respect it! I'd gone to Hyderabad for the Asian Social Forum, and I made a fake call from there to find out how things were at home. I was prepared for anything. Then I learnt that after I left, my father had a stroke, and he was hospitalized. Ma was fine. This was another guilt trip, but not that strong. Eventually when I visited home, it was an amazing welcome back. My father would call people and say that my daughter is back and she's doing great work!'

Meenakshi's father had his own roundabout way of reconciling matters. On learning that she and Jyoti lived together, he said it was wise indeed because Delhi was expensive and two or three people sharing a house made sense. Meenakshi was happy not to argue further. He also advised her to save something for the future. Her brother though was still not willing to accept her, but Meenakshi could not care less: 'I didn't care what he thought, I disowned him!'

The best part of the reconciliation was when Meenakshi's mother visited Delhi and spent a happy six months with her and Jyoti. 'She was treated like a *rani* [queen] of the house by both of us! She fell sick and we both took care of her. My office also joined us in looking after her and this experience was remarkable. My colleagues were no less than a very strong family to me!'

Unexpectedly, Meenakshi's mother did not pester her much about marriage. Instead, she shared her own unfulfilled aspirations, which she had never talked about to anyone. Meenakshi said she would forever treasure these moments. Within the next three years, she lost both her parents. Her visits to Kolkata became only about spending time with her elder sister, with whom she always had a close bond. There was also contentment in having reunited with her parents while there was still time.

Jyoti too had a reconciliation of sorts with her family around the same time, but it was a patch-up only with her mother who did not have much say at home. Her brothers, like Meenakshi's brother, still preferred that she stayed away, and she never returned to Kolkata. Meenakshi said she could not help but think at times about how Jyoti would be managing her life. But she had no way of finding out as Jyoti had left no avenues open for communication. Today, all she knows is that Jyoti still lives in the house they had bought together.

Parallel to managing her troubled relationship with Jyoti, Meenakshi rediscovered her friendship with Anish (name changed), her husband now and someone part of her and Jyoti's friend circle back in college in Kolkata. This was not the first time that Meenakshi felt attracted to Anish. Even as she was working out the biggest move in her life with Jyoti, she had found him engaging and there was a 'special corner' reserved for him in her heart. But it remained unspoken, and she had been sure about her love for Jyoti and commitment to move on with her.

On the Vexed Issue of 'Compulsory Marriage'

Veena Lakhumalani's experience: 'Once at Sujit's house, at a community meeting, a guy said he was going to get married, and everybody was ready to pounce on him. The question was: If I want to have a child what do I do? Then I have to have a wife. For me, as an outsider like a fly on the wall, it was a very interesting debate amongst themselves. From a human rights perspective he had a right to get married. And then I remember countering this same guy. I don't know how the topic came up, but the question was: What'd your wife do if she found out that you were gay? And he said, But I'm not being unfaithful to her, because I'm not having sex with another woman. And then I said, As a person who's not gay, but who's a woman, if you were my husband, I think if I found out that you were involved with another woman it'd be bad enough, but if I found out that you were gay and you were having sex with another man, then for me it'd be a much bigger blow. And I told him that you may not understand, but from a woman's perspective, this is much worse . . . But then on another occasion, I went with some of you to another gay man's house—he was married, he and his wife had a child, and she knew about it. Her thing was: Okay, now I'm married to this guy, what can I do? . . . And I said to this guy: Let's put it the other way—suppose I was a lesbian and I married you, and you discovered I was having a relationship with another woman, what'd be your reaction? He kept quiet, he didn't have an answer.'

Counsel Club meetings saw heated debates on the issue of including married gay men in the group. There was distrust even for bisexual men, married or not. But there was a rough understanding that a balance had to be struck in the interest of inclusiveness. While some gay and bisexual men did get married unthinkingly or for rather selfish reasons, there were many others who were genuinely unable to ward off the pressure from their families. At the same time, there were some, even if very few, who were transparent about their sexual orientation to their spouses and their marriage was not necessarily based on a compromise by either spouse. There was also recognition of the social pressure on the parents of queer individuals to have their children married off. This issue was taken up by Swikriti, a Kolkata-based queer support group that started in 2003, when they organized a series of meetings in 2005–07 for the 'significant others' of queer individuals. On these occasions, the families, friends and colleagues of queer people got an opportunity for a heart-to-heart chat with mental-health professionals, lawyers and queer activists to clarify their concerns and, above all, create support for one another.

The institution of marriage did not spare the allies of queer people either. Veena faced speculations about her sexual orientation because she was *not married* and *working with queer people*. Similarly, Dr Sherry Joseph had to assure his father about his intentions to get married: 'When I got engaged with Linu—it was an arranged marriage—I told her that I'm involved in social work and working with queer people. Her reaction was positive because she too had some good friends from the community. But my father used to ask me before marriage why I wasn't getting married. I'd say it was because of my PhD and job. Yet he'd ask me if I was "one of them". He'd even say that if I was, then we should think differently. So I often had to reassure him.'

Meenakshi started communicating more with Anish since 2008, with the understanding that she was still with Jyoti (even if it was about being separated under one roof). Around then, she took time off for about a year, to be on her own, and to figure out the next steps.

She needed to deal with burnout at work as well as the guilt that wracked her about doing 'injustice' to Jyoti. To make matters more difficult, it was Jyoti who had introduced Anish to Meenakshi in college, and even at that time a certain spark between the two had not gone down well with Jyoti. With the revival of their connection, matters became 'more unhealthy' as Meenakshi saw it.

The hiatus helped her clear her mind and take a number of decisions, including starting a new chapter with Anish in 2010. She was quite stumped to discover that all this while he had been a silent admirer of hers and never considered marriage himself. After Meenakshi left Kolkata, he went off to work in Nagaland. But he had been in the know through common friends of how her life was going, and not for once did he come across as judgmental about her sexuality and life choices in any way.

Perhaps Meenakshi had an apprehension about how I would react to her story. More than once she sounded a trifle apologetic talking about her relationship with Anish and her polyamorous identity. But when I shared similar personal sto-

ries, she felt reassured and spoke frankly. She disclosed her
intense desire to be a mother, which could not be fulfilled with
Jyoti because she was not ready to adopt a child. She questioned
whether the social ideal of 'perfect' one-to-one romantic and
sexual relationships was at all real and realistic. She was all gig-
gles when she recollected Anish proposing half in jest that all
three of them—Jyoti, Meenakshi and him—should try living
together. She was sure Jyoti would not have entertained the idea
one bit.

What prompted the decision to marry Anish? Meenakshi
was upfront about it: 'I could've had a live-in relationship with
Anish—and in fact that was the plan to begin with. But I was
tired of fighting. There would have been the inevitable social
pressure again—questions, raised eyebrows and all that. I just
didn't have the desire or energy to fight society once again.'

Does her marriage make Meenakshi a sell-out for the queer
cause? I can imagine many voices being critical of her move—
either openly or under a more sophisticated garb. But what
should be the ultimate test of success for any social movement
that seeks to free people from the shackles of restrictive gender
and sexual norms? Can queer movements prescribe a script of
'linear queering' for the people they engage with? Or should
their mandate be only to enable people to develop and act on
their own convictions, for better or for worse?

At the same time, there is something patently unfair in that
society should, on the one hand, create insecurities around anything beyond so-called norms, and then, on the other, offer the
institution of marriage as a way out—an institution that is itself

grossly unequal as it stands today and which often proves to be little more than a temptation. Can marriage really offer respite from fatigue? Can queer movements afford to stop questioning the inevitability of marriage even as they uphold an individual's right to work out their own survival strategies?

When Meenakshi and I decided to call it a day and wind up the interview, she said she had an incredible feeling of lightness. Then for a moment, she turned interviewer and asked me my side of the story in helping her and Jyoti escape to a new life. Apart from describing the thrill and energy I had felt, I remarked that the faith they had reposed in us had helped Ranjan, me and Counsel Club grow richer in experience. I recollected the rakhis they sent me and Ranjan in August 1997, as also the time I visited their one-room rented home in Delhi in March 1997 with Ranjan and one of the local queer activists who had helped them find their footing in the city.

Among the three of us, I looked closest to being Meenakshi's brother—a role I had to take on to pre-empt the landlady's curiosity about three men as visitors. Not only was I not to speak in English, none of us was supposed to utter a word that could have made the landlady suspicious about the couple. It was tricky to say the least but there was a reward in the form of delicious puris and kheer for dinner!

It seems incredible now that this was the last time I met Meenakshi and Jyoti together. Delhi was not too far from Kolkata, but travel was not frequent for me till some years later. Then there were the challenges of surviving without full-time employment, dealing with family pressures, working out romance, and the ups and downs of activism. Among the last mentioned was receiving a Customs Department show-cause notice in mid 1997 for distributing *Trikone* in India, a magazine on South Asian lesbian, gay, bisexual issues published from the US, which, the notice claimed, was 'derogatory to the morality and social system of our nation'. That would be another story, another time. But how much has changed in the way the state deals with matters sexual?

The Supreme Court of India finally read down Section 377 of the Indian Penal Code for good on 6 September 2018 and, in a much-celebrated verdict, delivered decriminalization to queer people. Much as one commends the apex court for upholding constitutional morality over social morality in its verdict, this change was unjustifiably delayed and long overdue (see Section 377 legal battle timeline later in this volume). And what of the laws around sex work, vagrancy, decency and obscenity that still criminalize queer people? What about the discrimination in terms of compulsory heterosexuality in-built into family, property, housing, insurance and labour laws? (Dhall 2018) Going by the continuing stories of harassment faced by queer people at the hands of the police and legislations such as the Transgender Persons (Protection of Rights) Bill, 2019, the question that arises is: Will the judiciary's openness change the attitudes of the legislature and the executive?

In effect, socio-legal stigma still forces many queer people to live parallel lives, which they must then make sense of and celebrate through a variety of innovations. These include not just queer support groups and journals but also the rainbow pride marches that today happen across dozens of towns and cities and attract tens of thousands as participants. Kolkata's

Friendship Walk in 1999 with just 15 people was possibly the first of these events (Siddhartha 1999). Today, these parades are so often seen as markers of the 'success' of Indian queer movements. But they also point at the existence of deep-seated and persistent social inequities that may well lead to another narrative such as this one quarter of a century from now.

PERSPECTIVES

Interview with Dr S. K. Guha

Professor of Tropical Medicine and Medical Superintendent cum Vice Principal, Calcutta School of Tropical Medicine, and Chairperson, ART Technical Resource Group, National AIDS Control Organisation, Delhi

Dr Guha's interactions with the queer communities (particularly transgender women and gay and bisexual men) largely began around the year 2000. But he has been associated with the national HIV response since 1998, and has closely seen the progress of the National AIDS Control Programme through the years. I first met him in 2006 while working with SAATHII, and since then have counted him as among the very few healthcare providers who can be trusted not just for his deep knowledge in his areas of work but also for his openness to queer people and concern for their well-being. This trust developed over numerous referrals of queer people to him to address their HIV and other health concerns.

I interviewed Dr Guha to understand how he saw the queer movements in West Bengal as a healthcare provider, and the changes he saw over time in how the health systems engaged with queer people. Within his rushed schedule, I could sneak in only three or four

questions over phone and email. The responses were rather econom-
ical but still provided some insight into the queer movement's engage-
ment with HIV concerns.

On the inclusion of MSM and transgender women in the national HIV response: It started in 1999 when the second phase of the National AIDS Control Programme was launched (DAC/ NACO 2011). One of the key policy initiatives was to scale up HIV-targeted interventions among most vulnerable groups in states where there was high prevalence of HIV. This helped bring in a focus on MSM and transgender populations.

Comparing the HIV Testing Scenario for Queer People in the Early 1990s with Current Times

Veena Lakhumalani recollected: 'I remember that some of the Counsel Club members wanted to get tested for HIV [in the mid 1990s]. And Sujit [Dr Sujit Ghosh] and I looked at each other and said, But why? I said, If you're [infected with HIV], it's too late, and if you're not, what do you need to do to protect yourselves? Once you do that you don't need to get an HIV test.' Somewhat dated advice now, but it was relevant then.

This was almost a decade before HIV testing and treatment options were readily available and even longer before they were better accessible in India. At that time, the emphasis used to be entirely on prevention of HIV and care and support for those already infected. People were routinely advised to first identify a support system of friends, family and healthcare providers before going in for an HIV test. This was easier said than done because of the all-pervasive stigma and myths associated with HIV *and being queer.*

In many ways it was the nascent awareness and sensitization efforts of these times at family, community, health systems and policy levels that later became the building blocks of solidarity for the HIV and some sections of the queer movements.

On his interaction with queer people and what their primary concerns are: My interactions are limited to clinical care of MSM and transgender people living with HIV, including counselling services, management of opportunistic infections [illnesses that occur when HIV affects the body's immunity] and anti-retroviral therapy [treatment that helps contain the spread of HIV infection in the body].

People in the initial years were more hesitant to disclose their HIV status as well as sexual orientation and practices. Over the years subtle changes have taken place. In the tertiary-care hospital where I work, HIV-status disclosure to medical doctors doesn't seem to be a problem for most people living with HIV as they are counselled by trained counsellors in HIV testing centres.

Sexual-orientation disclosure to doctors has improved. But in general, LGBT people are more concerned about stigmatization and discrimination in the healthcare settings around their sexual orientation rather than their HIV status.

On the engagement of queer movements in Bengal with health systems for tackling HIV: I'm not very sure about the engagement part, but in my view the reach [of the movement] has to be enhanced considerably among students, healthcare personnel, politicians, industries, and law and policy makers. The general population as well, more so in the rural areas.

Recognition of their identities and rights is the most fundamental issue. Stigma-free environment, especially in healthcare settings is crucial. Among health needs, the focus has to be around HIV and mental health.

Dr Sherry Joseph on His Experience of Research among Queer Communities in the 1990s

In 1995, I was in Delhi University and that's where I selected the topic of working on concerns of MSM for my PhD. Getting registered in Delhi University was something I never thought would happen because they had very strict, stringent criteria. I was very lucky that I had a good supporter, Prof. R. R. Singh, who later became the director of Tata Institute of Social Sciences, Mumbai. He was my research teacher also, and he was a supporter of qualitative research. He said we should do case studies and that should be more than enough for a PhD.

Initially I was thinking of focusing on HIV issues because of my earlier interactions with activist group AIDS Bhedbhav Virodhi Andolan in Delhi. They were fighting forceful testing of sex workers for HIV. So that's where I had my basic information, knowledge and records from. I still remember the Wednesday-evening meetings at Indian Coffee House on Baba Kharak Singh Marg. So I'd decided to work something out on HIV, and then also something on marginalized populations. At that time I wasn't sure. That's when I started researching on LGBT issues, and an outcome of that was an article in the *Economic & Political Weekly*. By that time I had an idea of what was happening all over the country, and a bit about the politics between gay and lesbian groups. That was when many lesbian voices were coming up.

Things were hectic in Delhi being part of the faculty as well as conducting my research. Then I got an opportunity to teach at Visva-Bharati University in Santiniketan, and I felt I'd be able to do both teaching and research better there. But I'd no idea about the distance between Santiniketan and Kolkata. When I realized that the distance was nearly 250 km, it became a nightmare! It'd be a question of making train trips such that I could go over to Kolkata during the day, finish what I had to do [interactions and interviews with queer individuals associated with Counsel Club or other queer groups and networks], stay the night at a friend's place or elsewhere, and be back early next morning to take my classes.

This experience was good, because when we teach social research we say that we have to be with the people, understand the context. Otherwise normally researchers are paper researchers—you'll find a person, you'll conduct an interview, and then take whatever information you want. But qualitative research gave me a very different experience. That actually is a wealth. I had 10 case studies, and these were very long in-depth case studies. I don't know how many times I followed back with each of the interviewees, because every time you transcribe these interviews, you discover a gap. And that time it was all pen on paper, so I had to write it down and mark the gaps. Some of the interviewees even got fed up because of my follow-ups! So in the end I think I had 14 cases that were key to my thesis, before I edited them further and converted them into matter for my book (Joseph 2005).

At that point of time, qualitative research was new for the discipline of social work. Otherwise it was 100, 200 or 500 interviews [a more quantitative-research approach], or you do a purely secondary data analysis . . . Conventionally in India people think that for a doctoral degree you need to have a minimum of [quantitative] database. But qualitative research offers new approaches. It helps when everything you're studying is unique in itself.

Among the problems I faced in trying to collect data for my research was non-inclusion. I was very open wherever I was going and declaring my research interest. I'd no sexual interest. My research was participatory in nature in the sense that I was engaged with the processes that were taking place, whether it was a party or a central group meeting or the sharing of an experience. Initially, my entry was difficult, especially in the Delhi groups. When they came to know that I'm an external person, they questioned why I should be allowed in. I think they had internally a debate on this issue. There were also people who really helped me out—Anjali Gopalan, Shivananda Khan, Ashok Row Kavi—those who understood the value or the worth of the work. Probably they gained confidence in me because of my articles. They may have thought I was non-threatening, while other groups perhaps thought that I'd use any information against the community or present it in a distorted manner. So there was resistance. I wanted to help and empathize with the community, but I wasn't being able to.

Much later, I remember Anand Grover [human rights advocate associated with Lawyers Collective, Delhi] telling me, We're filing your book for the hearings on Section 377 of the Indian Penal Code in Delhi High Court. This was in early 2001.

As a university-approved product in a researchable area, it must've been useful to them as a supportive document [for their arguments against Section 377 in a public-interest litigation filed by the Delhi-based Naz Foundation (India) Trust in 2001, the second petition in a long line of legal battles waged against this law across a quarter of a century]. And this is something that Lawyers Collective did on its own. So I'm happy that somebody found some use for the work I've done. And then I always felt that if I collect data, I must do something useful in return. Converting the data into a paper or a book to make it more widely available seemed the best thing to do.

[Sherry's contribution to queer movements as a researcher seems all the more laudable when one loses count of the researchers assisted by groups like Counsel Club in terms of information, data and contacts, who never reciprocated with a copy of their work or even by just keeping in touch.]

An 'Outsider's' Account: Conversation with Dr Paul Boyce

Senior Lecturer in Anthropology and International Development, University of Sussex, UK

Paul came in touch with Counsel Club in 1996 during the first of his visits to India for research on sexualities, HIV and human rights. He started attending the group's fortnightly meetings and other events, and developed a rapport with the group members. This association grew into bonds of friendship, which have lasted till date. While not as much a frequent visitor to India and Kolkata, any more, his attachment to this part of the world remains strong and is now reflected more in his writings and long-distance research collaborations with academics and activists in India. In a Yahoo

Messenger chat in January 2018, he shared a detached but ringside view of the multiple queer movements that Bengal witnessed since the 1990s, including their 'meeting points' and 'tensions'. Excerpts:

101

OUT OF LINE
AND OFFLINE

On his career and developing the India link: I work as a lecturer in anthropology and international development at the University of Sussex. I did a PhD in gender studies at the London School of Economics, and an MA in applied anthropology at Goldsmith College, University of London—during which I first came to Kolkata. I worked for many years as a consultant in community-based HIV, sexualities and rights research for development agencies. I also pursued post-doctoral research based in India.

The first time I came to India I went to Delhi to work at the Naz Project there [headquartered in London and led by Shivananda Khan, among the earliest South Asian queer activist voices, the Naz Project focused on sexual-health services for MSM]. I recall that Debanuj [associated with the Kolkata chapter of Naz Project and a Counsel Club core-group member then] was there at the time and he suggested I come to do some work in Kolkata and I agreed. In fact, I'd written to both chapters of Naz from the UK (sending and receiving letters!) after a class on HIV and sexualities in India during my MA. I'd met Shiv in London after that class and the seeds of the plan to come to India as a component of my MA had been sown then.

On his affinity for Calcutta . . . Kolkata: It was very different to Delhi. Certainly the Naz Project [in Kolkata] was very nascent and as a project there seemed more for me to do. I worked with Deep [in charge of the Kolkata chapter and also a member of Counsel Club in the early years]. We developed our first funding application to the West Bengal Sexual Health Project [one of the first government-aided projects of its kind in India in response to the emerging HIV epidemic]. When the money came through, Deep asked me if I'd stay on and I thought I would.

I think the city offered both a space for work and a space for refuge in an odd way. In some part at least, it was on the outer rim of globalization at that time, so there was something of an alternation to the pace of one's life. We have seen that change over the last 20 years, and I remember intense conversations about the emergence of those changes at the time. Plus personally I think being in Kolkata allowed me to be very involved in something—the work—at the same time as being a bit cut off, in a new place, a new life . . .

On what he saw of the diversity in the queer movements in Bengal: I recall the spaces of queer organizing and emergence then— Counsel Club, Classic Books [an 'alternate' bookstore in central Kolkata that stocked copies of *Pravartak* and *Bombay Dost*], the emergence of Pratyay [in 1997–98 as a support forum for transgender women and now one of the oldest groups of its kind in India], the British Council sponsored events, and other less centrally visible formations and ways of organizing. Plus also the social and cruising spaces of the city.

About the less centrally visible formations, I came to know people in Bongaon, for instance. There the locus of organizing wasn't so centred on Kolkata, and in a way seemed to be hesitant about the kind of associations emerging in Kolkata. I recall that a group of people there went off to Nabadwip in search of a memorial to a Vaishnavite devotee named Lalita Sakhi who was male-bodied but would wear a sari [some Vaishnavites in Bengal wear a sari while performing *sadhana* for Lord Krishna in *sakhi bhava*]. In a way this was about orienting away from seemingly metro queer formations into other spaces and figurations. I guess there were different ways of being going on at once, that shared lots of partial but not whole connections. There was no singular queer movement per se.

In places like Bongaon, things like queer support groups may've been perceived as from another kind of urban, or perhaps middle-class social world—these were perhaps also seen to demand forms of unwelcome or unfamiliar visibility. One of the newer criticisms of the queer movement in India has been for its emerging out of purely middle-class spaces. I'm not sure I agree with that entirely. I take the point but . . .

Certain class issues may be true—for example, the predominance of English in organizing spaces and publications at the time. But I think there were other points of activism though. Was CC [Counsel Club] so entirely middle class, for example? Even if it was to begin with, it did diversify over time. I think even in early days people like Ranjan were making those connections.

On whether there came to be a sameness to different queer movements in Bengal: I think there's still sameness and difference going on. There are different points of orientation [see story later of Sudeb Sadhu and formation of Prantik Bongaon, a support group of transgender women, in 1999–2000].

On frictions between different strands of the queer movements in Bengal: I think that was very palpable at the time. The main divide was between an ambivalence about explicitly claiming queer- or LGBT-type forms of recognition in Praajak [an NGO focused on sexual-health services provision which grew out of the Naz Project in Kolkata][19] versus the seemingly more 'out' forms of recognition in CC. Then there was also the poetics and politics associated with these approaches. The politics was also for a while worded as 'sexual health' versus 'human rights', but those merged over time. [Though not mentioned by Paul, over many years there were overlaps between Praajak and Counsel Club at the level of several individuals being associated with both organizations—this was even as the two agencies often disagreed publicly in their approaches to addressing the concerns of queer communities].

On where the queer movements have arrived today: Well, last year [2016] was my first time in the city in ages. I see a lot more diversity in the movement—regional voices, vernacular voices, much more clearly present and contesting some of the contours of the movement. I see the evacuation of funding—the loss of HIV monies—in some measure being a curtailing factor. [In recent years many governments and donors worldwide have reduced HIV funding support, which has been criticized as an ill-timed move given that the epidemic has far from ended, particularly among marginalized communities and in the Global South.]

On the impact of the movements at a personal level: My association with the queer movements in [West] Bengal has come and gone. I mean the years of my close involvement are somewhat in the past—as they must be, being older now, not living there

---

19 Praajak has now evolved into an NGO that works with children, adolescents and young adults in the areas of child neglect, abuse, exploitation and the juvenile-justice system in urban and rural West Bengal. In a broader sense it addresses issues around masculinities and gender equity.

and so on. Yet in recent years, I have returned to my involve-ment there much more intensely again, in writing projects and so on.

So the lasting imprint turns out to be foundational in a way—a part of myself that I still turn to, and wonder about what was I doing there? How did that come about? I think the involve-ments have been pivotal in ways that I'm only now coming to understand. I feel a bit of a proxy, since it's not 'my' movement or context but in so many ways I feel enmeshed and defined by those experiences. I think we all do. It was a very special time, a coincidence of many things.

Among the books I'm working on is one called *Sexualities, HIV and Ethnography: Sexual Worldings and Queer Misrecog-nitions in India*—this'll centrally focus on work in Bengal and looks at ways in which queer life-worlds may not be empirically evident, and what that means for HIV and sexual rights initia-tives. An edited book called *Research, Sex and Sexualities* will be out soon—this is more sociological in focus. I'm also writing a piece of a special edition on *Kolkata Characters* in which too I look back at 'those times' and wonder about the past as it rushed in the present and vice versa. Stories of past are always of the present . . .

On the next visit to Kolkata: I'm returning there a lot in my mind lately—to the place and time. The past seems more relevant in the present than it did at the time. I think it's in the air, with new developments in HIV and queer politics. Plus it's our age. We're at the time of looking back in wonder . . . I might come to Kolkata for my 50th birthday.

Sudeb Sadhu's Story: A Different Take on Relationships and Community Building

Also known as Suvana Ritu (a name adopted as part of a specific relationship and used mostly on Facebook), Sudeb is a 38-year-old transgender woman who lives in Baruipur, south of Kolkata, but spends weekends with her parents in Bongaon, her birth place—a town on the India–Bangladesh border. At one time she was a senior outreach worker with MANAS Bangla, a network of queer CBOs which ran one of India's largest HIV interventions for MSM and transgender women across West Bengal from 2004 to 2011. Today she works as a community-mobilization, data-collection and project-evaluation consultant to NGOs and government agencies. Our conversation was split over two meetings—the first in September 2017 and the second in late December the same year.

Sudeb was never particularly interested in studies, but this was not a worry or deterrent for her. Currently in the process of medical gender transition, she is also playing the lead female role in a film being made by friends—'If psychologists and surgeons can help me become a woman, why can't I be one in the world of films? Why should people like me play only comic roles?' The film will be a tribute to the transgender community in Bengal, which she feels helped her reach where she is today.

In her adolescence, which was during the initial emergence of queer movements in Bengal, Sudeb was fortunate to have supportive parents who quietly accepted the 'variance' in her gender and never came down on her for not acting 'like a boy' (both she and her brother were dressed in 'girly' clothes in early childhood, though he is neither transgender nor gay). She did become aware of her 'difference' in society's eyes as she grew up, but that did not stop her from mixing with other young people in the neighbourhood. Sometime in 1995, she also started making friends who were 'like her', but it was only in 1997 that she first got hint of an entire movement around the 'difference' that marked her personality. She chanced upon a book on *hijra* communities *Bharater Hijrah Samaj*, till date among the few well-researched books in Bengali on queer issues. It was written by two academics Ajay Majumdar and Niloy Basu, who were both Bongaon residents, and one of them (Ajay Majumdar) was her neighbour.

Sudeb became a key figure in the formation of Prantik Bongaon, a support forum for transgender women, as she gradually became aware of the social and sexual networks of transgender women and the men interested in them (sexually and romantically). This was in 1999–2000, and through the efforts of Kolkata-based NGO Praajak, with whom Niloy Basu and his co-author had already connected as part of their research. Sudeb too had approached Niloy Basu along with her friends for advice on setting up a support forum. Praajak brought all parties together for an initiative that was among the first of its kind beyond urban India.

I met Sudeb in 2001, when she worked on a sexual health study for Integration Society, Counsel Club's sister NGO. Over the years, as I worked further with her (including during my work in SAATHII), I saw her grow into a community leader fiercely protective of her fellow community members, whether in the workplace (in MANAS Bangla) or in the larger community in Bongaon. When she was posted in Baruipur during her

Sudeb Sadhu (centre) conducting a dance rehearsal with members of queer support group Astitva Dakshin in Baruipur, *c.*2007. Photograph courtesy Sudeb Sadhu.

tenure in MANAS Bangla, she became instrumental in the running of Astitva Dakshin, a local queer support group. Always a voice of reason, and despite having worked with several queer groups, she says she is detached and does not believe in playing favourites.

Quite a raconteur, she shared many gems on her friendships, and how Prantik Bongaon came to be. Even after years of knowing her I was unaware of many of these incidents. Here's one example: 'In Bongaon, apart from just one community friend in school, I used to see four or five hijras moving around together. I knew they were like me, but they were far more mature and I was confused if they were hijras. In the meantime, my sexual and romantic life made a start. But the best part was when after my school finals in 1995, during a train trip with my cousin to Dakshineswar, I discovered that Dum Dum Junction [railway station] was a hugely popular socializing and cruising site for my community members! This opened new doors for me and I became a regular visitor.

'There used to be three large age-wise groupings—ours was interested mainly in *adda*. The discovery of Dum Dum led to the realization that all train routes meeting at the junction, including the Kolkata Metro Railway, were popular cruising zones. Gradually, all stations up to Bongaon also became popular. Over time, I became very attached to the place—it was like a motherland—and with the friends I made there. Even after so many years, the junction's still popular as a meeting point, but not as much since 1998, when there was some major trouble that scared away people.

'When Dum Dum became out of bounds, I thought of befriending people in Bongaon. As I mixed with transgender women in my home town, I felt that so many of us were lonely and looking for partners. Around this time I'd broken off with my first romantic partner, and realized that such relationships weren't the most important thing to fret about. I wanted others also to realize that most men they were yearning for were never going to be their "fixed" partners. So, along with one of the first community friends I made, I started a trend of swapping sexual partners. This actually helped break the ice and brought people together as a community!

'This led to weekly community picnics—we'd gather at a friend's place and have fun with dressing up, singing and

ABOVE AND FACING PAGE. Sudeb at her residence in Baruipur. *Photograph by Prosenjit Pal.*

dancing. Our network grew. Even at this stage (early 1999), there was no thought of forming a formal group. Then for different reasons we had to stop our gatherings at the two places that were accessible. The next effort was to popularize a spot near Ichamati River. But this was a public place where we couldn't have expressed our emotions freely. So we thought of hiring a room for our meetings. The idea was speedily dropped because we couldn't imagine anyone renting out their space for people like us. This led to the decision of approaching Niloy-da and Ajay-da, who already knew many of us. They helped us find an advocate's room which became available once a month for our meetings and recreation. Then they too joined in. Gradually

we became aware of [Kolkata's] pride walk, Praajak and other groups like Pratyay, Counsel Club and Integration Society.

'These were the first steps towards forming Prantik Bongaon and registering it. Initially there was confusion and apprehensions about the objectives. But we decided it'd be a group that would provide support even to the families of the members. If someone's family member fell sick, we'd go in twos and threes to visit them. We became the talk of the town, with people wondering why we'd gotten together . . . There were also some situations of distrust when activists from Kolkata visited us. Many people in Bongaon didn't understand what "gay" stood for. Most of us identified as *kothi* [feminine men who often play a receptive role in sexual relations with other men] and the perception was that if two men have sex, then one has to be feminine and the other masculine. There were other factors as well that had to be dealt with—cultural, geographical and religious differences. As we interacted with more and more people, many of the doubts and distrusts were resolved. But even today some people still frown upon anything beyond their own gender or sexuality!'

On the impact of the queer movements on her life, Sudeb said: 'I have gained in self-confidence. Though I had family support, the pressure of marriage was there. My mother was very persistent but I always knew I didn't want to marry. Meeting so many queer people over the years gave me confidence and I could eventually convince my family members to look at things from my perspective.'

A Fellow Storyteller's Account of a Movement Maturing: Conversation with Sandip Roy

Journalist, Radio Broadcaster, Former Editor of *Trikone Magazine* and Author of the Novel *Don't Let Him Know*

I have known Sandip since 1991, the year I finished my graduation, which makes him the interviewee I have known the longest in this collection of stories. We became pen pals through queer newsletter Paz y Liberacion *published from San Jose in the US—we were both among the very few Kolkata names to be seen in the pen-pal classifieds. At that time Sandip worked as a software engineer in the US and it was much before he started volunteering with Trikone, the world's oldest-surviving South Asian queer support initiative that started in San Francisco in 1986. I first read about Trikone in* India Today *in the late 1980s, during my college days.*

FACING PAGE. The cover of an issue of *Trikone Magazine*, edited by Sandip Roy.

trikone MAGAZINE

Lesbian, Gay, Bisexual & Transgender South Asians

January 2002 · Vol. 17, No. 1
U.S.A. $3.95 · Canada $4.95
India Rs. 25

SEXXX!

Sandip immigrated to the US from India in the 1980s for reasons of career, but also with the hope of finding greater scope for freedom of expression as a gay person. Little did he know then that one day he would be contributing to starting a queer movement back in India, including his home town Kolkata. I met him on one of his trips to Kolkata in 1991, when one evening he took me along to a popular cruising site in South Kolkata, a public park. This was the first time I'd been in such a site—it looked pretty and mysterious like any other moonlit park would, just that the men were more interested in other men (yet another story, for another time).

During this trip Sandip also put me in touch with Siddhartha Gautam (1965–92), an advocate from Kolkata but then based in

BELOW AND FACING PAGE. Issues of and inside pages from *Trikone Magazine.*

Delhi. Siddhartha did pioneering work through his association with
activist group AIDS Bhedbhav Virodhi Andolan to make queer
issues prominently visible in the human rights discourse in India.
For Sandip, me and many others in our generation, Siddhartha's
labour of love was Less Than Gay: A Citizens' Report on the
Status of Homosexuality in India published in November 1991,
just months before he passed away (ABVA 1991).

Among the very first publications of its kind in India, this report
was by far the first that dealt so intensely with the details of queer
life in India from several angles—personal stories, culture, health,
law and more. Nicknamed the Little Pink Book (after its cover-page
colour and impact disproportionate to its small size), it also figured
along with Siddhartha in my conversation with Sandip in October
2017 at a restaurant in Salt Lake. Excerpts:

On where the queer movements in India have arrived: When I look at the movement now, I don't think I could've imagined back in the late '80s or early '90s that we'd be here, even talking about a project like this, that a project like this would be funded by a mainstream organization, and that this would be possible even as something like Section 377 still stands in the country [that is, at the time of the interview].

I remember in the early '90s when the famous *Little Pink Book* came out from ABVA, at the end of it there was a charter of demands for equal rights, marriage—I don't remember all of it. But at that time it had felt almost fanciful. In a country where I couldn't even fathom the thought of how to come out to my parents, and Section 377 was already there, but even beyond it there was no cultural space for it, where the only references at that time to homosexuality in India were newspaper reports of Rock Hudson dying of HIV—it was something so alien that I didn't even have the vocabulary to talk about it with my parents. In that scenario to talk about anything more than about not getting beaten up or beyond 377 seemed unimaginable. So in that sense, to see the cultural acceptance today—at least in a certain level of society, in the class I come from—is sort of astonishing.

On the fleeting gains made so far: The shift [in attitudes] in India has come about remarkably easily in a certain way. It sort of fell into place, court orders have been favourable, there hasn't had to be a Stonewall movement, people haven't had to take to the streets protesting police brutality, all of which has happened, people have been killed. . . but in general by virtue of class, a middle-class or upper-middle-class gay person has gained a lot of rights, visibility and sociocultural acceptance. Which in the

FROM THE ARCHIVES

The little pink book

• The heading refers to one of the most valuable documents in Counsel Club's collection of books and journals. A book smaller in size than this journal. With the main title set in a not-so-bold typeface on a modest pink cover. And the printing inside far from reader-friendly. Nothing to make it stand out. Except for its name which has never failed to spark off a gleam in many a "gay eye".

"Less Than Gay : A Citizens' Report on the Status of Homo- sexuality in India" – published by the New Delhi-based AIDS Bhedbhav Virodhi Andolan (see profile under Nos amis, page 22) in November 1991 – is indeed a "little book" with a "big deal" about it. Meticulous in its presentation of facts, unrelenting in its questioning attitude and thorough in its arguments, it has served as a treat to many minds starved for a book that would deal with homosexuality in an sympathetic manner.

Though not the first

Less than Gay

Dedication : This report is dedicated to the

A report on the '*Little Pink Book*' in *Pravartak*, January–July 1997 issue.

US they had to really fight for, in the '60s and '70s. We [in India] haven't really needed to have a gay rights movement in that strict sense. It was already an established concept outside and we plugged into it. So it has happened far more smoothly than I would've imagined in a culture as tradition-based as ours.

At the same time, the pitfall was that we took things for granted. So when the Supreme Court reinstated Section 377 [in December 2013] it took so many people by shock. Everyone felt that since the government decided not to defend the law [after the Delhi High Court ruling in 2009 that first read down Section 377], things must be done and dusted. People were planning gay businesses and gay tourism companies, so then it came as a rude shock to people when the law was reinstated. This also pointed at how fragile and tenuous our gains were, how dependent things were on just two judges who passed the verdict.

On the successes in changing the media narrative: I think one of the enormous success stories of the queer movement in India is how well it used, thought about and worked with the media in changing the narrative from one of either dismissal or derision to something that was somewhat more engaged. This came about not just because of gay people in the media but because of a general sensitization of the media, which is quite remarkable even without the existence of something like a GLAAD, which is an advocacy organization focused on media in the US. The movement figured out that one of the ways to change the media narrative was actually to expand it.

So whether it was Voices Against 377 [a unique collective of civil-society organizations working on children, women and queer people's rights that emerged in 2006] or parents of gay people going to the Supreme Court [asking for Section 377 to be removed], including people like late queer activist Nishit Saran's mother or screenwriter Chitra Palekar—all of these had a larger emotional resonance with the audience (Ravindran 2011). So when the 377 verdict [of December 2013] came down, and one of the judges used the term 'minuscule minority' for queer people in India [to justify reinstating Section 377], it got a huge amount of editorial space in almost every major newspaper in the country, no matter what its ideology was, and the matter wasn't dismissed as something irrelevant. This was at least true of the English media. And on television talk shows, virulently homophobic voices have almost disappeared as no one really wants to be seen as holding antiquated views on queer people.

Internet revolution—comparison with the early days of *Trikone* Magazine: Probably the biggest change that happened was the Internet. When I was growing up and coming out to myself, I knew obviously that there were other gay people in a country or city as big as this. But I had no idea of how to access any of them. Even if that was a time when people met each other in cruising parks, you still had to know which park to go to; someone had to tell you about it.

When *Trikone Magazine* started in the US, I remember one of the first exciting things was when they published a map of India and showed how many subscribers they had in different parts of the country, and Calcutta at that time had two, and I knew I was one of them! I remember writing to them asking if they could tell me who the other person was, and of course, they said: We can't, but you can put up a personal ad and maybe that person will contact you. And then there was this whole thing about how to put out a personal ad with your address on it, because getting a PO box in India was very difficult. And then after you've put in the personal ad, you spend so much time running down to catch the mail before anyone else in the house could get to it . . .

When I put in an ad, I had naively thought that only people in Calcutta or visiting Calcutta would contact me. But I had not understood how pent up and isolated so many people were. So that people who had no chance or intention of even visiting, whether they were in Punjab or someone going to school in

In the Beginning ...

An interview with Trikone founder Arvind Kumar

By SANDIP ROY

Almost every reader of Trikone knows it was started by **Arvind Kumar**. Though his fingerprints are all over Trikone, there is very little about him in it—no profiles, no coming out stories, no pictures. Our 10th anniversary provided a perfect excuse to chat with the man who started it all, to find out what it was like in the "old days."

While growing up in India did you ever wish there was a gay group there?

At the time, I didn't feel the need for joining a group. I was going through life from experience to experience. But there was also a lot of pain involved. I am sure if I had known about groups like Bombay Dost, it would have helped to know that I was not the only one with these crazy thoughts. A lot of times, my partners didn't want to "dwell" on it and make a big deal of it. I always felt I was abnormal for taking it ~~so seriously when~~

[San Francisco Gay Pride] Parade, I went up to their booth to say hello, but the people there didn't seem to care much.

One person I did meet after the parade was M.J. Talbot. We had a wonderful conversation on the sidewalk for over 45 minutes. And he got involved with GAPA (Gay Asian Pacific Alliance) which formed soon after.

The other resource was *Pacific Bridge* which reincarnated later as *Passport Magazine*. It was basically a cross-cultural Asian-non-Asian publication. But once again that space was heavily East Asian dominated. To their credit, they regarded me as Asian and printed a couple of my pieces. Still, the amount of space they gave to South Asian issues was very, very limited.

How did Trikone get known in India?

Arthur Pais got one of our press releases while he was working for *India Abroad* in New York and decided to do a story about ~~us~~

'95 [in San Francisco] with pictures of his wife and children would be received very well.

Who was the first South Asian gay man you met?

It was not through Trikone! I was an avid reader of the Advocate Classifieds, and in one issue I found this little note from a gay Indian guy. So I wrote to him and it turned out to be Suvir who lived only 15 miles away! When after several years of knowing him, I found our circle of friends hadn't grown, I snared him into forming Trikone, and we did the first few issues together. What I didn't expect was that so soon after forming Trikone I would meet Ashok [Jethanandani, Arvind's partner].

After you met Ashok, you never felt inclined to fold up Trikone and settle down in domestic bliss?

I did settle down, but I didn't form the group just so I could meet someone else, though I was ~~sure it was a motive somewhere~~

Sandip Roy's interview with Trikone founder Arvind Kumar in the tenth-anniversary issue of *Trikone Magazine*, January–March 1996 issue.

Manipal, they all just needed to write to somebody. That urgency to reach out to people was enormous and it went beyond hook-ups and sex. It was just the thrill of receiving the letters, of knowing there was someone else like them—in some ways it was exciting because for the first time you felt that there was a larger community out there even if you didn't really know how to access it. The Internet radically changed all that. It broke down all barriers. It made it easier and easier, and then the apps started.

It may be debatable whether the connections made through apps are more lasting, whether it's harder to actually build friendships that'll last long. But the Internet also triggered more ways for like-minded people to come together and created a different kind of activism that wasn't limited by geography.

On the contradictions that persist: There are enough tragic stories still happening. For example, the woman doctor in AIIMS who committed suicide because she found her husband, also a doctor, was involved in gay relationships. I was shocked because he was a doctor in 2015 who wasn't able to not get married, and then his wife kills herself because she can't think about the idea of divorce (Narayanan 2015). At the same time the generation of my nieces and nephews is far more cool about the idea, being queer isn't such an issue for them.

On the impact of 'accidental activism': I still don't think of myself as an activist in a certain sense, but for many of us in the early days, we became 'accidental activists' just because of where we were at that time—we were editing a magazine or whatever, it wasn't something we were thinking of as a career or even a major part of life. And for many of us at that time, even after going abroad, it was about finding other people who were also gay, with whom you could be yourself.

People were looking for partners, sure, but beyond that they were also looking for some kind of a community, friends, people to hang out with, as simple as that, and some of the activism came out of that. Because you were hanging out together, you engaged with each other, and when an issue came up you could mobilize around it. But in the early '90s if someone had told me that to be fully involved in these kinds of issues I would need to work with hijras, for instance, I would have freaked out! Hijras were the closest thing to alternate sexuality that I knew, and as somebody who was trying desperately to pass and not be caught out, I was always terrified that any attention from a hijra would reveal my reality to my family.

But today when I go to a queer party in a hotel or perhaps a nightclub, the kind with an entry fee, what is interesting to me is how much more of a class mix has happened, where there are persons from small towns, transgender people, and all kinds of people who I would normally not meet in my social life. Whereas when we were starting out, we weren't looking to cross class lines at all. The segregated circle of earlier days has been blown over by the sheer numbers that you see at the pride parades, and you can't have a party that is limited to a certain income bracket. A cover charge or location can act as a certain filtering agent, but only to a certain extent. At the end of the day you can't refuse anyone.

On the current political environment and its implications for the queer movement: I think there are a lot of different issues. I have friends who think that the LGBT movement should stick to LGBT issues, they don't need to take on larger political issues, they don't have to have a position on Kashmir or Dalit students or other forms of discrimination, they should just focus on queer issues—this runs contrary to movement-building ideas, of solidarity with other minority groups, and unless you do that it's never going to be a two-way street . . . I guess it's not very different from the US where you have organizations like the gay Republicans and the gay Democrats.

So, if there is a gay movement that is allied to the [political] right in this country, the BJP, I think that is great, because in the end, for the LGBT cause, that is a good thing; whether it's good for the country or not is an ideological stand that people need to take . . . One of the big things in the early days of the movement was that we wanted to keep saying that we're not freaks, we're just like you, we have the same problems, and this is, in fact, that thing come back to us, where we say we're just like everyone else—some of us are right-leaning, some are left-leaning, just like the larger population.

It just so happens that in a particular political party, whether it's the BJP here or the Republican Party in the US, if the top brass is stridently anti-gay, it becomes a much harder position for you to take, because you might believe in that party's ideology in terms of economy or nationalism, and yet you know there is a fundamental part of you that the party is inimically opposed to.

But otherwise we have to accept the fact that there'll be all kinds of people, and that gays won't be in some kind of ideological straightjacket. It's just like the fact that while it's an LGBT movement, the lesbians will have their own issues, their own needs, their own requirements for their own space and agenda. So there'll be points of confluence, but there's not going to be one happy rainbow family. It has never been the case or ever will be. This is something we have to accept as part of the maturation of the movement.

OVERLEAF. Letters from Counsel Club's files.

type of irrational

Dear Paw

Club

19

NOT ... CHILDREN ALLOWED

... WRITE FOR ... IN ADVANCE

SENDER'S NAME AND ADDRESS

12.9.95

... (Member)

... uncile club ...

Homosexual

In Continuation

In just about a year since my conversation with Sandip, queer people in India were no longer criminalized under the archaic Section 377. This had come to be after a chequered legal battle of more than 25 years (see timeline later)—the earliest legal challenge against Section 377 being mounted in the early 1990s by activist group ABVA through petitions to the Parliament and Delhi High Court. Given the Supreme Court of India's ruling in August 2017 on the right to privacy as a fundamental right and its observation that sexual orientation was an essential attribute of privacy, there were strong indications that this statute would eventually be struck down, or at least read down as it once was by the Delhi High Court in 2009 before being inexplicably reinstated by the Supreme Court in 2013 (Divan 2017).

After the last round of Supreme Court hearings on Section 377 concluded in July 2018 on an optimistic note, reading down of this section seemed like a done deal. Moreover, the judges[20] seemed inclined to look at the impact of Section 377 in an expansive sense—beyond criminalization of penile non-vaginal sexual intercourse to the undermining of queer people's constitutional rights to equality, non-discrimination, privacy, dignity and freedom of expression (Saxena 2018). This sensibility prevailed in the landmark 493-page verdict of 6 September

---

20 The 6 September 2018 Supreme Court verdict on Section 377 (*Navtej Singh Johar and Others v. Union of India*) was issued unanimously by a five-member constitution bench consisting of the then Chief Justice Dipak Misra and Justices R. F. Nariman, D. Y. Chandrachud, A. M. Kanwilkar and Indu Malhotra.

2018, in which the court conclusively read down Section 377 to decriminalize adult consensual sexual relations in private, irrespective of the sex or gender of the persons involved. It also paved the way for queer people to claim a greater stake to their constitutional rights in future.

It is but fitting that the concluding thoughts of many of the narrators in this story, shared long before the Supreme Court verdict was out, dwelt around the future stakes for queer people in (eastern) India and what the queer movements should be engaged with. Some, like Veena, were unhesitatingly generous in their overview of the queer movements: 'If I really reflect on the last 30 years, I think there have been quite a number of significant changes. The fact that the print and electronic media cover LGBT issues, mainstream films are covering issues like these . . . there'll always be the guys and dames who think this isn't what India's all about, which is a load of rubbish. If you go to our temples and paintings and see what happens there, it's all there for the whole world to see. I think 20–30 years down the line, things will change significantly. And then people like yourselves and the other groups can look back with pride and say, we were the torch bearers, we were the pathbreakers!'

Other interviewees like Sherry were more critical: 'I stand by what I said in the past as well, when I said that the gay and lesbian movement would be sidetracked by the HIV movement. That was part of the driving force for this movement. It came out of the health issue, globally and in India. This was a good opportunity for the LGBT communities to take advantage of HIV and then do more, but unfortunately it wasn't done. When I look back I still think that many things were achieved, no doubt about it, but organized, collective alliance building, these were things missing. The movement took some strides and matured but it should've done more. Everyone was behind the law [Section 377], too much emphasis on it, and too many expectations that the law would bring the heavens to your doorstep. But it'll never happen even if you have a good law or policy. Social attitudes need attention, as do issues of employment, for instance, the example of Kochi Metro providing employment to transgender people.'

Meenakshi echoed Sherry on what approaches queer movements should embrace: 'I really can't detach myself from the larger human rights movement, especially the women's movement. I think we're in a transitory phase. People are now able to enjoy their rights more and more, but many of the core [problem] issues are intact. So a huge challenge is to do something innovative to keep those issues alive in people's minds.'

Sherry's point on employment, or inclusive livelihood options, relates to the Supreme Court's emphasis on constitutional rights in its verdict on Section 377 and has already been gaining traction among queer activists. Meenakshi takes the issue of constitutional rights to a more fundamental level—the issue of legal backing for non-discrimination around gender and sexuality diversity in every sphere, including recognition of queer relationships: 'In the last 20 years we've moved from the closet to visibility—the queer movement is now visible within the larger human rights movement. But for the future, the biggest challenge for the queer movement is the legal one. Sometimes having laws maybe a problem, but not having a law that recognizes our relationships as something very organic is a huge obstacle. If such a law existed, then it wouldn't give some

powerful people the right to interfere in our lives and to persecute us.'

Meenakshi's suggestions resembled the Supreme Court's
in another regard—that of the need to familiarize and sensitize
the larger public to queer issues: 'The other issue is how do we
bridge the gap in communication? We need to be creative such
that people at large are able to understand that issues of gender
and sexuality are part of our human evolution. Why should
what Ismat Chughtai wrote years ago be discussed only in a certain class or circle?'(see Chughtai 1990).

Among all the interviewees, Sudeb perhaps was the most
introspective and self-critical: 'Wherever I've reached today, even
this interview being taken, is an outcome of whatever happened
so many years ago. On the other hand, sometimes I feel very
lonely. That may be because I have understood matters so deeply
that I've moved away from everyone. Even my old friends in
Bongaon think twice before speaking to me. Maybe I too have
become rigid in my ways, but it's not *ahankar* [arrogance].

'The movement that I saw as I was growing up is no longer
there. It's almost as if we've got all that we wanted and there's
nothing more to do. The tsunami of the late '90s and early
2000s has dissipated. We're now bothered only about our pro-
fessions. I'll work on issues of my gender or sexuality, but I
won't be part of a movement—I'll play safe. The hunger we had
has finished . . . We're happy that we can now dress up as we
like, and chat on social media inside a closed room. The cruising
sites that we were so eager to go to at the end of the day to meet
and speak to each other are no longer there. Is this the price we
have to pay for easy access?

'People have become so self-centred. Others before us sweated it out, but we don't want to stick out our necks any more. There's no thought for the future. This is nothing but a reflection of the direction in which the larger society is moving . . . We need a fresh crisis to galvanize ourselves again—away from these sexual-health projects that have reduced 'responsibility' to 'just work'. We need to be back on the path of questioning society, instead of functioning in a heterosexual framework of marriage and children, and being happy with the crumbs thrown at us by the government.'

Aparna too spoke about not being taken in by the state, but her tactics would be different: 'The future is still positive. I'm confident that the bill on transgender rights won't get passed. Even if it does, we should use it to get into the Parliament and change the law from within!'

Meenakshi and Sandip talked also about issues that tend to get lost or go uncontested in the general business (and busyness) that queer movements often cloak themselves in. Meenakshi shared: 'During our initial days in Delhi, there were a couple of informal get-togethers that we attended. That was the first exposure to the group of women who identified themselves as women lovers. There was something that made both me and Jyoti uncomfortable. Everything was centred on sex . . . it was more about how sexually can you be expressive, how comfortable you're talking about it. We were not. Even between us it wasn't the centre of our relationship. And politically I don't use the word 'L' because many people have a very narrow understanding of it. Even with feminism people have similar issues, and we do challenge such thinking. But I'm just not comfortable with the word [lesbian] because it's so centred on the [sexual] act. It's a very small part of two people loving each other . . . I could never associate myself with any of the queer women's groups in Delhi or Kolkata. We were always closer to a mixed group of women . . . I would urge the queer movement to not centralize the issue around sex.'

Sandip spoke about an issue that may alienate many queer individuals from the queer movements and the 'queer scene' in general: 'This might be nostalgia, about growing up in harder times, when you were more alone. But you did value the people you met in a certain way because you knew that these were people hard to find, and you invested a certain value in them. Whereas now—because of mobile apps and because there are so many people around all the time—it's become easier to discard people. Growing up as a queer person, my biggest fear— and this was a fear my parents had when I came out to them— that I might end up being lonely. I sometimes worry whether this plenitude of opportunities that one finds in apps makes people any less lonely. And the earlier groups that offered supportive spaces are gone. You're no longer getting together to stick stamps on envelopes and mail them, so neither are you in the process making friends the way you used to . . . And it's harder getting older as a gay person in India with fewer spaces where you can hang out, spend time together and keep in touch. So sometimes I wonder where have all the people I met in the 1990s gone.' This is clearly something that the queer movements have not quite taken into account.

When I flip through the files of letters received by Counsel Club, I too wonder where their authors are today—somewhere in India, in a different country or just around the corner from where I live. Perhaps some of them never went anywhere but cannot be 'seen' anymore because they have chosen to withdraw into the isolation they had emerged from, or into the 'security' that social norms seem to offer. Or should one blame it on Facebook and our capitulation to its charms? If you are not on it, do you not exist? And with its brute and manipulative archival capacity, perhaps you are visible only in the way and to the extent Facebook deems it. Though to be fair, it is also true that over the years Facebook did enable some happy reunions with long-lost friends, including a few of the narrators in this story.

This makes me think if I have done any better than Facebook. Have I done justice to the stories extracted from the Counsel Club archives or shared by the narrators and retold here? I hope I have. For eventually it is individual life stories that possess the strength to reflect and shape social move-ments—even if the movements sometimes like to believe that they wield the pen that writes and rewrites social histories.

377. **Unnatural offences:** Whoever voluntarily has carnal intercourse against the order of nature with any man, woman or animal shall be punished with imprisonment for life, or with imprisonment of either description for a term which may extend to ten years, and shall also be liable to fine. **Explanation:** Penetration is sufficient to constitute the carnal intercourse necessary to the offence described in this section.

1992	Civil rights group ABVA files a petition in Parliament for repeal of Section 377 but petition is never brought up for discussion
1994	Doctors associated with Delhi's AIDS-control programme attending health day event in Delhi's Tihar Jail find large number of inmates engage in male-to-male sex; the doctors recommend distribution of condoms; Kiran Bedi, Inspector General (Prisons), Delhi, vehemently denies existence of homosexuality in Tihar and says condoms will actually encourage immoral behaviour and go against law; ABVA files petition in Delhi High Court, argues Section 377 is barrier against public-health interest in distribution of condoms and should be scrapped; petition is not pursued consistently and ultimately dismissed by court by early 2000s

2001	Sexual-health outreach workers and queer activists associated with Lucknow-based NGOs Bharosa Trust and Naz Foundation International arrested under charges of abetment in relation to Section 377; offices of both NGOs raided by police; activist Arif Jafar incarcerated for 54 days before managing bail with support from Lawyers Collective
2001	Naz Foundation (India) Trust files petition in Delhi High Court challenging constitutionality of Section 377 on grounds of the law denying queer people their fundamental rights to equality, non-discrimination, freedom of speech and life
2006	Voices Against 377 civil-society collective files intervention supporting Naz Foundation stating that Section 377 violates fundamental rights of queer individuals—intervention includes six individual affidavits, making it the first time when queer individuals directly join legal battle in court
2009 (2 July)	Delhi High Court delivers judgement in Naz Foundation case by reading down Section 377 to exclude all consensual sex among adults in private—irrespective of gender or sex of individuals involved
2009	First special leave petition (SLP) filed within a few days in Supreme Court by astrologer Suresh

Kumar Koushal challenging Naz Foundation judgement; subsequently 15 other SLPs filed to oppose Naz Foundation judgement, a majority of them by religious outfits

2010–11   Five interventions in support of Delhi High Court verdict filed by mental-health professionals, parents of queer people, academics and others in the Supreme Court

2013 (11 December) Supreme Court in *Suresh Kumar Koushal & Another v. Naz Foundation & Others* reverses Delhi High Court verdict on decriminalization; upholds constitutionality of Section 377, thereby recriminalizing queer lives

2014   Review petitions filed by the Government of India, Naz Foundation, Voices Against 377 and other petitioners in Naz Foundation case rejected by Supreme Court

2014   Curative petitions filed soon after by the petitioners (barring Government of India) with key argument that Criminal Law (Amendment) Act, 2013 had decriminalized consensual non-peno-vaginal sex among adult men and women, thus making criminalization of consensual adult male-to-male sex under Section 377 constitutionally untenable (on grounds of right to equality)

2014 (15 April)   Supreme Court declares verdict on transgender rights in *National Legal Services Authority (NALSA) v. Union of India & Others*; acknowledges transgender identities within and beyond gender binary; says all Indian citizens have right to self-determine gender; issues directives to government on reservations and equal opportunities in education, livelihood, health, social welfare and overall well-being for transgender people; queer activists claim verdict contradicts and weakens basis for earlier ruling by the same court on Section 377

2016   Supreme Court admits curative petitions, refers them to five-judge constitution bench for further consideration on grounds that they deal with matters of constitutional importance

2016   Writ petition filed in Supreme Court by Navtej Singh Johar and four other queer individuals, all public figures in spheres of art, journalism, hospitality and business, arguing that Section 377 violated their rights to equality, non-discrimination, privacy and dignity

2016   Writ petition filed in Supreme Court by transgender activist Akkai Padmashali and other trans persons arguing that Section 377 violated their citizenship rights as acknowledged by Supreme Court's NALSA verdict by subjecting them to relentless persecution in the shape of harassment, physical abuse and sexual violence, and by criminalizing their choice of sexual/romantic partners

2017 (24 August) Supreme Court passes right to privacy judgement—in *Justice K. S. Puttaswamy & Another v. Union of India & Others* court says privacy is a fundamental right, and its own verdict reinstating Section 377 in December 2013 was a 'discordant note' in rights jurisprudence of Supreme Court; fact that Section 377 was not even a key matter for consideration before the court and yet it opined on it was a huge morale booster for queer activists and allies

2018 Supreme Court lists Navtej Singh Johar's writ petition as a matter to be heard by a five-judge constitution bench (but decides not to hear prior curative petitions at this stage because of certain limitations and asks those who filed curative petitions to file interventions instead)

2018 Additional writ petitions challenging Section 377 filed by hotelier Keshav Suri, Avinash Pokkaluri and other students and alumni of Indian Institutes of Technology, and queer activists Arif Jafar, Ashok Row Kavi and others. Intervention petitions filed by Naz Foundation, Voices Against 377, parents of queer persons, mental health professionals, and academics

2018   Final arguments and hearings conclude within a
                 week's time and matter reserved for judgement

2018 (6 September) Supreme Court reads down Section 377 to
                 restore status of decriminalization achieved
                 after Delhi High Court ruling in 2009; judgement
                 goes beyond decriminalization to uphold princi-
                 ples of constitutional morality which can be
                 crucial for further socio-legal campaigns for
                 non-discrimination on grounds of sexual orien-
                 tation and gender identity; judgement also
                 confirms principle of 'progressive realization of
                 rights', which means apex court's verdict will be
                 irreversible

ABVA (AIDS Bhedbhav Virodhi Andolan). 1991. *Less Than Gay: A Citizens' Report on the Status of Homosexuality in India*. New Delhi: ABVA. Available at: http://bit.ly/2GkwbGk (last accessed on 19 July 2019).

Banerjie, Ajita. 2017. 'In Rage, and in Hope, We Fight'. *Varta* (17 December). Available at: http://bit.ly/2GlAzVx (last accessed on 20 July 2019).

Basu, Sanjukta. 1999. 'Chhaichapa Fire' [Fire under Ash]. *Anandabazar Patrika* (3 April).

Bhugra, Dinesh, Kristen Eckstrand, Petros Levounis, Anindya Kar and Kenneth R. Javate. 2016. 'WPA Position Statement on Gender Identity and Same-Sex Orientation, Attraction, and Behaviours'. *World Psychiatry* 15(3): 299–300. Available at: http://bit.ly/2SlVtZq (last accessed on 19 July 2019).

British Council. 2000. *Human Rights Film and Cartoon Festival: A Report*. Kolkata: British Council.

Chughtai, Ismat. 1990. *The Quilt and Other Stories* (Tahira Naqvi and Sayeda S. Hameed trans). New Delhi: Kali for Women.

Das, Arnab, and Pawan Dhall. 2013. 'Culture and Issues of Rights to the Eyes of the Indians with "Other" Self-identities of Sexuality and Gender'in Subrata Sankar Bagchi and Arnab Das (eds), *Human Rights and the Third World: Issues and Discourses*. Lanham, MD: Lexington Books, pp. 235–64.

Siddhartha, Chitra. 1999. 'Gays Stage Friendship March'. *The Times of India* (3 July).

Dasgupta, Piyasree. 2011. 'Same-Sex Relationships: Punished in Life, Death'. *Indian Express* (28 February). Available at: http://-bit.ly/2JQui5o (last accessed on 19 July 2019).

DASGUPTA, Rohit K., Pawan Dhall. 2017. *Social Media, Sexuality and Sexual Health Advocacy in Kolkata, India: A Working Report*. New Delhi: Bloomsbury India.

DAC/NACO (DEPARTMENT OF AIDS CONTROL / NATIONAL AIDS CONTROL ORGANISATION). 2011. *More and Better: There's No Looking Back—NACP-IV Working Group Meeting—MSM Sub-group Report: Version 2–5 May 2011*. New Delhi: Ministry of Health and Family Welfare, Government of India.

DHALL, Pawan. 2014. 'Queer Developments in Odisha'. *Varta* (July). Available at: http://bit.ly/30LYhmf (last accessed on 16 August 2019).

DHALL, Pawan. 2018. 'How Campaigning Has Contributed to the Decriminalization of Homosexuality in India'. *SOGI Campaigns* (5 November). Available at: http://bit.ly/2ZFJeZQ (last accessed on 16 August 2019).

DHALL, Pawan, and Paul Boyce. 2015. 'Livelihood, Exclusion and Opportunity: Socioeconomic Welfare among Gender and Sexuality Non-normative People in India'. *IDS Evidence Report 106*. Brighton: Institute of Development Studies.

DHALL, Pawan, and Soma Roy Karmakar. 2015. 'Qatha: Times and Lives of Girly Boys from '60s Kolkata (Parts 1–3)'. *Varta* (February–April). Available at: http://bit.ly/2HzzhXU; http://bit.ly/32ejfu5; http://bit.ly/34bIf73 (last accessed on 16 August 2019).

DHAMIJA, Chitralekha. 1998. 'Loving Women: Indian Lesbians Talk about Their Lives and Loves'. *Sunday* (17–23 May), pp 34–45.

DIVAN, Vivek. 2017. 'Dazzled, and Hopeful—The Notion of Privacy for all Indians'. *Varta* (August). Available at: http://bit.ly/2GrDY5k (last accessed on 24 July 2019).

DUTTA, Aniruddha. 2016. 'Undoing the Metronormative: Urban–Rural Exchange within LGBT Communities in Eastern India' in Pawan Dhall (ed.), *Queer Potli: Memories, Imaginations and*

Re-imaginations of Urban Queer Spaces in India.. Mumbai: Queer Ink, epub.

141

OUT OF LINE
AND OFFLINE

JOSEPH, Sherry. 2005. *Social Work Practice and Men Who Have Sex with Men*. New Delhi: Sage.

JOSEPH, Sherry, and Pawan Dhall. 2000. 'No Silence Please, We're Indians! Les-Bi-Gay Voices from India' in Peter Drucker (ed.), *Different Rainbows*. London: Gay Men's Press, pp 157–78.

LAHARIYA, Khabar. 2019. 'How Kumbh's Kinnar Akhada Is Changing Attitudes'. *The Wire* (1 March). Available at: http://bit.ly/3oO9BOw (last accessed on 30 August 2019).

NARAYANAN, Devesh. 2015. 'Is Just the 'Gay Husband' to Blame for This AIIMS Doctor's Suicide?' *Youth Ki Awaaz* (21 April). Available at: http://bit.ly/2ydnhWB (last accessed on 24 July 2019).

PARTHA. 1994. 'Prejudice Mightier than the Pen'. *Pravartak* (July–December), pp 5–6.

PATTOJOSHI, Amrit, Biswa Bhusan Pattanayak and L. Ramakrishnan. 2017. 'LGBT Mental Health: The Way Forward'. *Odisha Journal of Psychiatry* 25 (September): 2–8.

PHUKAN, Mitra. 1994. 'Soul Sisters'. *Miscellany: The Sunday Statesman Review* (3 July), pp 9.

RAVINDRAN, Shruti. 2011. 'My Son Is Gay, and I'm Proud of Him'. *Indian Express* (20 February). Available at: http://bit.ly/2y7FAwI (last accessed on 26 July 2019).

REDDY, Gayatri. 2005. *With Respect to Sex: Negotiating Hijra Identity in South India*. Chicago: University of Chicago Press.

SAMPOORNA. 2019. 'SPWG Statement on Transgender Persons (Protection of Rights) Bill 2019'. *Sampoorna* (19 July). Available at: http://bit.ly/2MNcBoO (last accessed on 17 October 2019).

SANJAY. 1997–98. 'Sunset or Sunrise?' *Naya Pravartak* (August 1997–May 1998), pp 7–10, 17.

SARIA, Vaibhav. 2019. 'Begging for Change: Hijras, Law and Nationalism'. *Contributions to Indian Sociology* 53(1): 1–25.

SAXENA, Shambhavi. 2018. 'This Is the Final Chapter against Section 377: Here's What Went Down in Court'. *Youth Ki Awaaz* (16 July). Available at: http://bit.ly/2YjrIKs (last accessed on 20 July 2019).

SEMMALAR, Gee Imaan. 2017. 'First as Apathy, Then as Farce: The Transgender Persons (Protection of Rights) Bill, 2016'. *Orinam* (14 August). Available at: http://bit.ly/2JHXY5P (last accessed on 20 July 2019).

SHARMA, Parvez. 1994. 'Emerging from the Shadows'. *Miscellany: The Sunday Statesman Review* (3 July), pp 6–8.

VANITA, Ruth, and Saleem Kidwai (eds). 2000. *Same-Sex Love in India: Readings from Literature and History*. New York: St. Martin's Press.

Many thanks to everyone who took time off from their present and went back in time with me to reminisce, revise my perception of how things were, laugh and cry over memories, accompanied so often over great food and drinks—Anubhav, Aparna Banerjee, Dr Paul Boyce, Dr S. K. Guha, Dr Sherry Joseph, Meenakshi, Sandip Roy, Sudeb Sadhu, Suresh and Veena Lakhumalani.

I am indebted to those I could not meet for a conversation, but whose courage has been an immense inspiration for me and no doubt will be for the readers as well—Jyoti, Mamata, Ryan, Monalisa, Sucheta and Swapna. Thank you to the SAATHII, Bhawanis and Santi Seva teams, and especially to Jaina Nani—you are an endless repository of stories still waiting to be heard and told. Any mention of Jaina Nani will be incomplete without mentioning her protégé and my colleague Amrita Sarkar for all the groundwork done with Santi Seva in Bhadrak.

I am ever so grateful to Svran Apeejay Journalism Foundation whose generous grant in their very first round of funding made it possible for me to reach out to many of the narrators in this story.

Thank you Seagull Books for your invaluable support—many years ago with providing space for *Pravartak* and its contemporary queer journals at the Seagull Bookstore, and now by publishing this story. How better to complete a cycle of history?

As I write this, I cannot help but remember so many of my partners in crime from the days of Counsel Club, Integration Society and *Pravartak*—without repeating those already named above and in keeping with the *Pravartak* policy of using only first names or aliases—CC founders KK, Parvez, Raj, Rinkoo, Sujit and Udayan; as also others who joined in along the way—Abhra, Aditya M, Amlan, Anis, Anupam, Aveek, Debanuj, Deep, Dominick, Gopal, Gulrez, Jaideep, Jayanta, Julia, Kiki, Kunal, Kushal, Madhuja, Navonil, Palash, Partha, Peter, Pia, Puppee, Rajarshi, Rana, Rohit, Sanjay, Sanjib B, Sanjib C, Santanu G, Santanu P, Souvik (the universal bro), Sudarshan, Sudip (*boro*), Sudip (*chhoto*), Sunita, Susanta, Sunayna and Tirthankar.

Rafiquel Haque Dowjah aka Ranjan, for you there should be a separate chapter. But here I will thank you only for livening up *Pravartak* visually, memorable first-time journeys all through Bengal and Odisha, and for the education I gained by travelling in the general compartments of Indian Railways with you.

No mention of Counsel Club, Integration Society and *Pravartak*'s work will be complete without acknowledging the support and critiques from my peers since the earliest years: Anindya Hajra, Arif Jafar, Arvind Narrain, Ashok Row Kavi, Bina Fernandez, Chayanika Shah, Debalina Majumder, Dr L. Ramakrishnan, Late Shivananda Khan, Late Siddhartha Gautam, Minakshi Sanyal, Mohan Gunatilake, Maya Sharma, Nitin Karani, Owais Khan, Paul Knox, Sridhar Rangayan, Suhail Abbasi, Vivek Anand, Vivek Divan and Yadavendra Singh. Or my guides and gurus through the years, rather decades—Late Kusum Gupta and her daughters Anuja Gupta and Sujata Gupta Winfield, Amit Ranjan Basu, Anand Grover, Anjali Gopalan, Ashwini Ailawadi, Dr Jangoo Kohiyar, Dr Sai Subhashree Raghavan, Dr Sujit Ghosh, Himalini Varma, Jolly Laha, Linu Joseph, Mira Kakkar, Santayan Sengupta and Sonal Mehta.

Thank you Sayan Bhattacharya for your ideas, patience, impatience and disturbingly keen insight—and not just in relation to this volume! Prosenjit Pal, thank you for all the steps taken together—you are in this story in more ways than you may realize, or I might! Thanks Shyam Balasubramanian for that phone call—the inspiration in those words was as valuable as the information. And to Vaibhav Saria—for all the time spent together in (discussing) academics, drinking, dancing and activism, which aptly sums up as *adda*!

To my Varta Trust colleagues, friends and contributors—heartfelt thanks for joining hands to bring *Pravartak* back through or as the *Varta* webzine, and the emotional support right through the writing of this story. I am grateful to my brother Uday Dhall, sister-in-law Rooma Gurwara Dhall, and nieces Udita and Ridhima Dhall for their constant encouragement; as also to Punita Kochhar Tadanki, Vinita Kochhar and Niranjan Tadanki; Pramodh Nijhawan; Sujata Absar; Alok, Sudha and Shilpi Bhattacharya; and the one and only Lakhi Bibi.

Of course, I have not managed to include everyone in the lists above, but only because I cannot afford to make this list longer than the book itself!

As always, remembering my loving father Prakash Chandra Dhall, who had no inkling what he was contributing to when he bought me that portable typewriter in 1991—the very same one on which *Pravartak* was first typed out. But where or how do I begin to thank you, Usha Dhall? You may not see me or catch my voice very well any more, but probably are the only one who *ever really* heard me.

OVERLEAF. Image from back cover of *Pravartak*, July–December 1994 issue. *Artwork by Tia.*

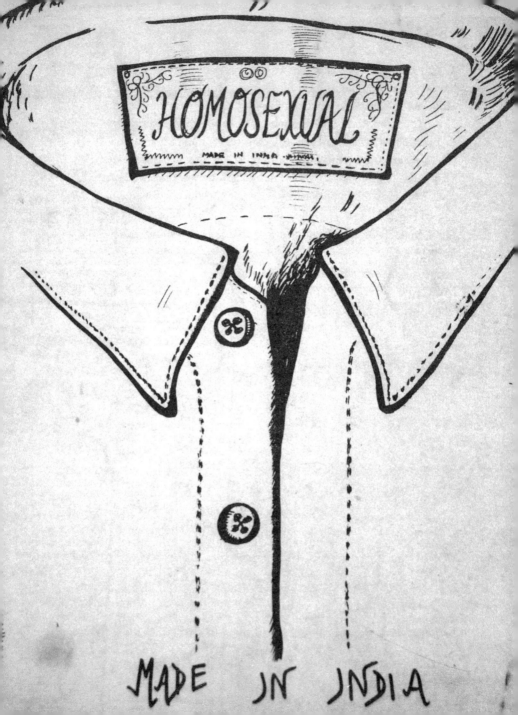